AF269637

SERIES ENDORSEMENTS

"There are so many fine commentaries available today, but it's great to have a reliable author you can turn to for solid Reformed reflections on Scripture. In this case, there are sixteen of them—friends and fellow shepherds who have given me great insight into God's Word over the years. I'm looking forward eagerly to each one of these sermonic commentaries!"

Michael S. Horton
J. Gresham Machen Professor of Apologetics and Systematic Theology at Westminster Seminary California
Host of the *White Horse Inn* Talk Show
Editor-in-Chief of *Modern Reformation* magazine

"Those of us who have promoted and practiced *lectio continua* expository preaching through the years eagerly await the volumes announced in the *Lectio Continua Expository Commentary on the New Testament.* We are equally eager to read such a series written by pastors who have practiced the method in their churches. The international and interdenominational character of the series will only add to the richness of its insights."

T. David Gordon
Professor of Religion and Greek at Grove City College
Author of *Why Johnny Can't Preach* (P&R, 2009)

"As the history of preaching is unfolded, it becomes clear how important the orderly, systematic preaching through the Scriptures has been, and why it has been a favorite homiletic approach over the centuries. One is surprised to discover how many of history's great preachers made a regular practice of preaching through one book of the Bible after another. Origen, the first Christian preacher from whom we have any sizable collection of sermons, preached most of his sermons on the *lectio continua.* We find the same with John Chrysostom who is usually referred to as the greatest Christian preacher. We find the same true of Augustine as well. At the time of the Protestant Reformation, Zwingli, Calvin, Bucer, and Knox followed this system regularly, and they passed it on to the Puritans. Today, we see a real revival of *lectio continua* preaching. *The Lectio Continua Expository Commentary on the New Testament* represents a wonderful opportunity for the Church to recover a truly expository pulpit."

Hughes Oliphant Old
Formerly John H. Leith Professor of Reformed Theology and Worship at Erskine Theological Seminary
Author of *The Reading and Preaching of the Scriptures in the Worship of the Christian Church* (7 vols., Eerdmans, 2007)

"The concept behind this series is a fascinating one and, given the list of authors, I am confident that the final product will not disappoint. This promises to be a great resource for churches seeking to know the Word of God more fully."

Carl R. Trueman
Professor of Biblical and Religious Studies at Grove City College

Second Timothy

THE LECTIO CONTINUA

Expository Commentary on the New Testament

Series Editors

Joel R. Beeke | Jon D. Payne

Other available books in this series:

- *Romans* — J. V. Fesko
- *First Corinthians* — Kim Riddlebarger
- *Galatians* — J. V. Fesko
- *Ephesians* — Ian Hamilton
- *Philippians* — David T. A. Strain
- *Hebrews* — David B. McWilliams
- *Revelation* — Joel R. Beeke

Second Timothy

Michael G. Brown

REFORMATION HERITAGE BOOKS
Grand Rapids, Michigan

Second Timothy

Reformation Heritage Books
3070 29th St. SE
Grand Rapids, MI 49512
616-977-0889
orders@heritagebooks.org
www.heritagebooks.org

All italics in Scripture quotations have been added by the author.

Printed in the United States of America
22 23 24 25 26 27/10 9 8 7 6 5 4 3 2 1

Library of Congress Cataloging-in-Publication Data

Names: Brown, Michael (Michael Grant), 1970- author.
Title: Second Timothy / Michael G. Brown.
Description: Grand Rapids, Michigan : Reformation Heritage Books, [2022] | Series: The Lectio Continua expository commentary on the New Testament | Includes bibliographical references.
Identifiers: LCCN 2021043199 (print) | LCCN 2021043200 (ebook) | ISBN 9781601789105 (hardcover) | ISBN 9781601789112 (epub)
Subjects: LCSH: Bible. Timothy, 2nd—Commentaries.
Classification: LCC BS2745.53 .B76 2022 (print) | LCC BS2745.53 (ebook) | DDC 227/.8407—dc23
LC record available at https://lccn.loc.gov/2021043199
LC ebook record available at https://lccn.loc.gov/2021043200

For additional Reformed literature, request a free book list from Reformation Heritage Books at the above regular or email address.

For my sons,

ISAAC and IAIN

From childhood you have known the Holy Scriptures, which are able to make you wise for salvation through faith which is in Christ Jesus.
—2 Timothy 3:15

Contents

Saint Thomas Church in Strausbourg,
where Martin Bucer exposited God's Word in 1523.

Preface

On a clear day, I can see the Italian Alps from the balcony in my study. Their impressive form stares at me like the imposing faces of majestic giants, sculpted by deep lines of gray and green, crowned with snow-topped peaks. Living in Milan, I know that the Alps are never far away. A map over my desk shows me their geographical proximity. But the fact is that most days I can't see them at all. They are usually obscured by the city's notorious *nebbia*, the foggy haze that completely washes out the horizon. Months pass before I can even manage to make out a few of the Alps's jagged lines. It is easy to forget that these breathtaking mountains are a present reality. Whenever they reappear, it is always a pleasant surprise.

Over the years I have had a similar experience with 2 Timothy. I am well aware that this short letter is in the New Testament, located between Paul's other two Pastoral Epistles, 1 Timothy and Titus. I am familiar with its contents and have preached and taught on it many times. Yet much like the joy I receive when the Alps reemerge from their hiding, I experience amazement when I read 2 Timothy in its entirety. This letter offers far more than pious advice for pastors (a noble thing in itself); it is nothing short of a devotional masterpiece. These are the last surviving words of an apostle who "fought the good fight...finished the race...[and] kept the faith" (4:7). It is a letter full of encouragement for believers in every age as they seek to live out their faith in a hostile world and bring the gospel to the next generation. Second Timothy is a lush valley in the green pastures of God's Word.

This commentary is based on sermons I preached in 2012 at Christ United Reformed Church in Santee, California, where I served as pastor from 2003 to 2018. The content was sharpened and refined, however, during the subsequent years as my appreciation for 2 Timothy continued to grow. It was particularly during the period of 2015 to 2018, while I wrestled with God's call to leave a beloved ministry and comfortable life in San Diego to serve on the foreign mission field, that I read, reread, reflected on, and prayed more deeply through this marvelous letter. In many ways, this commentary was hammered out by the Lord on the anvil of my own doubts and fears about the future. The outcome is an exposition of 2 Timothy that aims not only to be Christ-centered, redemptive-historical, and gospel-focused but also packed with pastoral and practical application. God willing, it can serve as a tool for a pastor while he preaches *lectio continua* through 2 Timothy, a resource for church leadership to read together, or devotional material for the individual Christian or prayer group. May God use what has been written in these pages to strengthen believers by the grace that is in Christ Jesus to endure suffering for His gospel and persevere to the end.

In writing this commentary, I sought to read broadly in the Christian tradition the vast scholarship on the Pastoral Epistles. Those whom I found most helpful include George Knight III, Philip Towner, John Calvin, Walter Liefeld, Donald Guthrie, Gordon Fee, Patrick Fairbairn, William Mounce, J. N. D. Kelly, and John Stott. I have also tried to incorporate comments from the early church fathers where applicable, as I believe firmly in the importance of showing the continuity between the Reformation and the ancient church.

I am grateful to my good friend and colleague Rev. Dr. Jon Payne for asking me to write this commentary and for his extraordinary patience while he waited for the manuscript! May you continue to preach the word, Jon, always being ready in season and out of season. I also want to extend my thanks to those who read the manuscript (or parts thereof) and offered helpful feedback, suggestions, and encouragement: Joel Beeke, J. V. Fesko, Simonetta

Carr, Chuck Tedrick, Brad Lenzner, Mark Patterson, and especially Barbara LaPointe. As always, I am indebted to my beloved wife, Janie, who is my biggest supporter and source of encouragement in my ministry both as a preacher and as a writer.

I have dedicated this book to my sons, Isaac and Iain. May our Lord strengthen you by His glorious gospel to fight the good fight of faith and finish the race.

Michael G. Brown
Milan, Italy

Series Introduction

The greatest need of the church today is the recovery of sound biblical preaching. We need preaching that faithfully explains and applies the text, courageously confronts sin, and boldly trumpets forth the sovereign majesty, law, and gospel promises of God. This type of powerful proclamation has vanished in many quarters of the evangelical church only to be replaced by that which is anemic and man-centered. Instead of doctrinally rich exposition which strengthens faith and fosters Christian maturity, the standard fare has become informal, chatty, anecdote-laden messages, devoid of instruction in the truths of the Christian faith. This approach leaves unbelievers confused and keeps believers in a state of chronic spiritual adolescence.[1]

There is indeed a dire need for the recovery of solid biblical preaching. Not only does reformation of this sort lead Christ's sheep back to the verdant pastures of His soul-nourishing Word, it also provides a good example for present and future generations of

1. A stinging, yet constructive, critique of modern-day preaching is found in T. David Gordon's *Why Johnny Can't Preach: The Media Have Shaped the Messengers* (Phillipsburg, N.J.: P&R, 2009). "I have come to recognize that many, many individuals today have never been under a steady diet of competent preaching.... As starving children in Manila sift through the landfill for food, Christians in many churches today have never experienced genuine soul-nourishing preaching, and so they just pick away at what is available to them, trying to find a morsel of spiritual sustenance or helpful counsel here or there" (Gordon, *Why Johnny Can't Preach,* 17). Elements of this introduction are adapted from Jon D. Payne, "The Roaring of Christ through *Lectio Continua* Preaching," *Modern Reformation* 19, no. 6 (Nov.–Dec. 2010): 23–24, and are used by permission of the publisher.

ministers. For this reason, we are pleased to introduce The Lectio Continua Expository Commentary on the New Testament, a new series of expository commentaries authored by an array of seasoned pastor-scholars from various Reformed denominations on both sides of the Atlantic.

What is the *lectio continua* method of preaching?[2] It is simply the uninterrupted, systematic, expository proclamation of God's Word—verse by verse, chapter by chapter, book by book—that endeavors to deliver the whole counsel of God (Acts 20:26–27). Christian discipleship is impoverished when large portions of Scripture are ignored. Carried out faithfully, the *lectio continua* method ensures that every passage is mined for its riches (even those verses which are obscure, controversial, or hard to swallow). Paul states that "all scripture is given by inspiration of God, and is profitable for doctrine, for reproof, for correction, for instruction in righteousness: that the man of God may be perfect, thoroughly furnished unto all good works" (2 Tim. 3:16–17 KJV).

Lectio continua preaching has a splendid heritage. It finds its roots in the early church and patristic eras. Its use, however, was revived and greatly expanded during the sixteenth-century Protestant Reformation. When Huldrych Zwingli (d. 1531) arrived at the Zurich Grossmunster in 1519, it was his desire to dispense with the standard lectionary[3] and introduce *lectio continua* preaching to his congregation by moving systematically through the Gospel of Matthew. At first, some members of his church council were suspicious. They were uncomfortable replacing the lectionary with this

2. In Christianity, *lectio continua* (Latin for continuous reading) originally referred to the practice of reading Scripture sequentially in public worship, as was the practice of the ancient church. This practice is recommended by the Westminster divines in the Directory for Public Worship, which, in turn, served as an impetus for *lectio continua* preaching. Sadly, Scripture reading in this manner has been neglected in Reformed and Presbyterian churches for many generations, perhaps as far back as the eighteenth century, when public worship was reduced to sermon-hearing sessions.

3. A lectionary is a plan or table of Scripture passages to be read in the services of church for each day or week of the year.

seemingly new approach. But Zwingli explained that the *lectio continua* method of preaching was not new at all. On the contrary, important figures such as Augustine (d. 430), Chrysostom (d. 407), and Bernard of Clairvaux (d. 1153) all employed this homiletical approach. Zwingli is quoted by his successor, Heinrich Bullinger (d. 1575), as saying that "no friend of evangelical truth could have any reason to complain" about such a method.[4]

Zwingli rightly believed that the quickest way to restore biblical Christianity to the church was to preach the whole counsel of God verse by verse, chapter by chapter, book by book, Lord's Day after Lord's Day, year after year. Other Reformers agreed and followed his pattern. In the city of Strasbourg, just ninety miles north of Zurich, preachers such as Martin Bucer (d. 1551), Wolfgang Capito (d. 1570), and Kaspar Hedio (d. 1552) practiced *lectio continua* preaching. Johannes Oecolampadius (d. 1531) boldly preached the *lectio continua* in Basel. And let us not forget John Calvin (d. 1564); between 1549 and 1564, the Genevan Reformer preached sequentially through no fewer than twenty-five books of the Bible (over two thousand sermons), which he was able to do because he also preached regularly for weekday services.[5]

The example of these Reformers has been emulated by preachers throughout the centuries, from the post-Reformation age down to the present. In the last half of the twentieth century, Donald Grey Barnhouse (1895–1960), Martyn Lloyd-Jones (d. 1981), William Still (d. 1997), James Montgomery Boice (d. 2000), and John MacArthur all boldly preached straight through books of the Bible from their pulpits. But why? Surely we have acquired better, more

---

4. It is interesting to note that the year before Zwingli began preaching sequentially through books of the Bible, he had received a new edition of Chrysostom's *lectio continua* sermons on Matthew's gospel. See Hughes Oliphant Old, *The Patristic Roots of Reformed Worship* (Black Mountain, N.C.: Worship Press, 2004), 195. Cf. Hughes Oliphant Old, *The Reading and Preaching of the Scriptures in the Worship of the Christian Church*, vol. 4: *The Age of the Reformation* (Grand Rapids: Eerdmans, 2002), and Timothy George, *Reading Scripture with the Reformers* (Downers Grove, Ill.: IVP Academic, 2011), 228–53.

5. T. H. L. Parker, *Calvin's Preaching* (Edinburgh: T&T Clark, 1992), 159.

contemporary methods of preaching? Is the *lectio continua* relevant in our twenty-first-century context? In a day when biblical preaching is being increasingly undermined and marginalized by media/story/therapy/personality-driven sermons, even among the avowedly Reformed, these are important questions to consider.

Shortly before the apostle Paul was martyred in Rome by Emperor Nero, he penned 2 Timothy. In what proved to be some of his final words to his young disciple, he wrote, "I charge thee therefore before God, and the Lord Jesus Christ…*preach the word*; be instant in season, out of season; reprove, rebuke, exhort with all long suffering and doctrine" (2 Tim. 4:1–2 KJV). This directive was not meant only for Timothy. It is the duty of every Christian minister (and church) to heed these timeless words; according to God's divine blueprint for ministry, it is chiefly through the faithful proclamation of the Word that Christ saves, sanctifies, and comforts the beloved church for which He died.[6] In other words, the preaching of the gospel and the right administration of the sacraments are the divinely sanctioned and efficacious means by which Christ and all His benefits of redemption are communicated to the elect. For this reason alone the *lectio continua* method of preaching is a helpful practice in our churches, providing a steady diet of law and gospel from the entirety of God's Word.

Some may ask, "Why another expository commentary series?" First, because in every generation it is highly valuable to provide fresh and reliable expositions of God's Word. Every age possesses its own set of theological, ecclesiastical, and cultural challenges. Thus, it is beneficial for both current and rising ministers in every generation to have trustworthy contemporary models of biblical preaching. Second, these volumes uniquely feature the expositions of an array of pastors from a variety of Reformed and confessional traditions. Consequently, this series brings a wealth of exegetical, confessional,

6. See Matthew 28:18–20; Romans 10:14–17; 1 Corinthians 1:18–21; 1 Peter 1:22–25; Westminster Shorter Catechism, Q. 89.

experiential, and practical insight, and furnishes the reader with an instructive and stimulating selection of *lectio continua* sermons.

This commentary series is not meant to be academic or highly technical. There are many helpful exegetical commentaries written for that purpose. Rather, the aim is to provide *lectio continua* sermons, originally delivered to Reformed congregations, which clearly and faithfully communicate the context, meaning, gravity, and application of God's inerrant Word. Each volume of expositions aspires to be redemptive-historical, covenantal, Reformed and confessional, Trinitarian, Christ-centered, and teeming with spiritual and practical application. Therefore, we pray that the series will be a profound blessing to every Christian believer who longs to "grow in the grace and knowledge of our Lord and Savior Jesus Christ" (2 Peter 3:18).

We are pleased to announce that this series of commentaries is now being published by Reformation Heritage Books, which graciously agreed to take over this large task from Tolle Lege Press. We thank Tolle Lege for printing the first three volumes (*First Corinthians* by Kim Riddlebarger, *Galatians* by J. V. Fesko, and *Hebrews* by David B. McWilliams). We, Joel Beeke and Jon Payne, look forward to coediting the remainder of the series for Reformation Heritage Books. The goal is to publish two volumes per year in the King James or New King James Version, according to the choice of each author.

In addition to thanking Reformation Heritage Books and its faithful team for producing this series, we wish to thank our churches, Christ Church Presbyterian, Charleston, South Carolina, and the Heritage Reformed Congregation, Grand Rapids, Michigan, for warmly encouraging us as ministers to work on projects such as this one that impact the wider church. Furthermore, we thank our dear wives, Mary Beeke and Marla Payne, and our precious children for their heartwarming support, which makes editing a series like this one possible. We both feel that God has greatly blessed us with God-fearing wives and children who mean more to us than words can express.

Finally, and most importantly, thanks and praise must be given to our blessed triune God, the eternal Fountain of all grace and truth. By His sovereign love and mercy, and through faith in the crucified, resurrected, and ascended Christ, we have been "born again, not of corruptible seed, but of incorruptible, by the word of God, which liveth and abideth for ever. For all flesh is as grass, and all the glory of man as the flower of grass. The grass withereth, and the flower thereof falleth away: but the word of the Lord endureth for ever. And this is the word which by the gospel is preached unto you" (1 Peter 1:23–25 KJV).

—Joel R. Beeke and Jon D. Payne, series editors

Introduction

Second Timothy may be the most underrated letter in the whole Pauline corpus. We typically do not show it the attention it deserves. This is somewhat understandable, given that this short epistle does not contain a majestic defense of the gospel as we find in Romans and Galatians or whole chapters of focused, doctrinal teaching like in 1 Corinthians, Ephesians, and Colossians. It does not even appear (on the surface, at least) to have the kind of practical education for the church that we immediately discover in Paul's other Pastoral Epistles, 1 Timothy and Titus, both of which include instructions concerning the qualifications of men who desire to serve in church leadership (1 Tim. 3:1–13; Titus 1:5–9).

Yet this little letter provides us with something that no other book in the New Testament does. It is Paul's last surviving piece of correspondence, offering us a glimpse of the aged apostle at the end of his life. After some thirty years of ministry, he has "fought the good fight…finished the race…kept the faith" (2 Tim. 4:7). He is incarcerated in Rome and facing the death penalty. He is lonely, cold, and without the necessary tools to redeem the time. Still, he is full of hope, for he knows that the crown of righteousness is laid up for him (4:8) and the Lord will preserve him "for His heavenly kingdom" (4:18).

Convinced that the time of his departure is at hand, Paul writes with a great sense of urgency to his young and trusted colleague Timothy. Paul had finished his race. Timothy must now carry the torch. He must *guard the gospel* against false teachers so that it would be brought to the next generation (1:13–14; 2:16–18). He must *entrust the gospel* "to faithful men who will be able to teach others also" (2:2). He must be willing to *suffer for the gospel* like his mentor (1:8, 12; 2:3, 9; 3:12; 4:5). Above all, he must *preach the gospel* and fulfill his ministry (2:15; 4:1–5). All of this makes 2 Timothy the most personal and intimate of Paul's letters. As Philip Towner put it, "From the perspective of the Pauline corpus, or the Pauline story, this is the final chapter."[1]

Second Timothy is also a letter full of timely instruction for the church today. Like Timothy, we live in "the last days" (3:1), when people are "lovers of themselves, lovers of money" (3:2), and "lovers of pleasure rather than lovers of God" (3:4). We live in a time when people do "not endure sound doctrine, but according to their own desires, because they have itching ears…heap up for themselves teachers" (4:3). We need leaders in the church who will "hold fast the pattern of sound words" given by the apostles and codified in the church's creeds and confessions (1:13). We need ministers who will "preach the word…in season and out of season" (4:2), who will "be watchful in all things, endure afflictions," and "do the work of an evangelist" (4:5). Second Timothy describes the world in which the church now lives, a world full of apostasy and godlessness. If the gospel and sound doctrine are to advance into the next generation, the church (especially ministers of the word and church leaders) must heed the exhortations and warnings found in this small book.

This letter is also full of encouragement for Christians as they seek to live out their faith in a hostile world. Like Timothy, we can become discouraged by our circumstances and be afraid to suffer for the gospel. Paul helps us understand that "God has not given us a spirit of fear, but of power and of love and of a sound mind" (1:7). He writes to us as a pastor, telling us to "be strong in the grace that is in Christ Jesus" (2:1). He tells us that we can be confident in Scripture, which is "given by inspiration of God, and is profitable for doctrine, for reproof, for correction, for instruction in

1. Philip H. Towner, *The Letters to Timothy and Titus*, New International Commentary on the New Testament (Grand Rapids: Eerdmans, 2006), 79.

righteousness" (3:16). He faithfully points us to Christ and comforts us with God's promise that He will award the crown of righteousness "on that Day, and not to me only but also to all who have loved His appearing" (4:8). Far from being a technical manual for pastors, 2 Timothy is teeming with practical application for every believer.

Authorship

The writer of this letter identifies himself as the apostle Paul (2 Tim. 1:1). There is no compelling reason for us to believe that this Paul was anyone other than the former persecutor of Christians whom Christ called to be an apostle (Acts 9:1–22). He opens the letter with a salutation (2 Tim. 1:2) and concludes with a benediction (4:22) in a formula consistent with all other Pauline letters. He refers to his appointment as "a preacher, an apostle, and a teacher" (1:11) and makes multiple references to his sufferings for the gospel (1:8, 12; 2:9–10; 3:11). He refers to Timothy as his "beloved son" (1:2; see also 2:1) and displays intimate knowledge of him, his family, and his ministry (1:3–6, 13–14; 3:10–11, 14–15; 4:13, 21). He presents God as the one who saves us "not according to our works, but according to His own purpose and grace which was given to us in Christ Jesus before time began" (1:9). This Christ "abolished death" through the cross (1:10), is now "raised from the dead" (2:8), and has given us "the Holy Spirit who dwells in us" (1:14). He exalts Scripture as the inspired word of God (3:16; cf. 2:9), which must be preached (4:2), followed (1:13), and defended (2:2, 15–18; 4:3–4). All this and much more bear witness to the internal evidence that 2 Timothy was written by the apostle Paul.

Additionally, the external evidence for Pauline authorship of this letter is very strong. Like the other Pastoral Epistles, 2 Timothy was regarded as Pauline in the early church. Allusions to the Pastoral Epistles are found in 1 Clement (ca. 96), the works of Ignatius (d. 108), Polycarp (d. 155), and Justyn Martyr (d. 165), and citations are made by Irenaeus (d. 202) and Clement of Alexandria (d. 211). The Muratorian Canon, a late second-century document that lists recognized biblical writings, ascribes 2 Timothy to the apostle Paul. Moreover, in the fourth century, the church historian Eusebius included 2 Timothy among the Pauline Epistles and as part of the New Testament canon.[2]

One exception to the early church's recognition of 2 Timothy as Pauline was the heretic Marcion's claim (85–160) that the Pastoral Epistles were not written by Paul.[3] Marcion rejected much of the Bible largely on the basis of his belief that the God described in the Old Testament is different from the one described in the New. He published his own list of New Testament books, eliminating all but ten of Paul's letters and a highly edited version of the Gospel of Luke. Marcion was denounced and excommunicated, but the church actually owes a debt to his heresy for at least two reasons. First, his claims forced the early church to respond with a scholarly defense of the New Testament canon. Second, they bear witness to "the traditional place which the Epistles to Timothy and Titus occupied in orthodox circles at Rome about the year 140."[4]

Paul's authorship of the Pastoral Epistles remained a steady tradition in the church until the nineteenth century, when Enlightenment theologians Friedrich Schleiermacher, Johann Gottfried Eichhorn, and Ferdinand Christian Baur called it into question.[5] Building on this criticism, academics such as P. N. Harrison have rejected Pauline authorship of the Pastorals largely on the basis that they present a historical setting that is difficult to reconcile with the

---

2. Eusebius, *The Ecclesiastical History*, trans. by H. J. Lawlor and J. E. L. Outon (London: SPCK, 1927), 3.3.5.

3. The early church father Tertullian (160–220) records this in his *Against Marcion* 5.21.

4. J. H. Bernard, *The Pastoral Epistles* (1899; repr., Grand Rapids: Thornapple Commentaries, 1980), xviii. For more documentation on the early church's acceptance of the Pastoral Epistles, see Bernard's introduction, xi–xxi; George W. Knight III, *The Pastoral Epistles: A Commentary on the Greek Text* (Grand Rapids: Eerdmans, 1992), 13–14; and Towner, *Letters to Timothy and Titus*, 3–9.

5. See Friedrich Schleiermacher, *Über den sogenannten ersten Brief des Paulos an den Timotheos* (Berlin: Realschulbuchhandlung, 1807); Johann Gottfried Eichhorn, *Historisch-kritische Einleitung in das Neue Testament* (Leipzig: Weidmanischen Buchhandlung, 1812); and Ferdinand Christian Baur, *Die sogenannten Pastoralbriefe des Apostels Paulus aufs neue kritisch untersucht* (Stuttgart: Cotta, 1835).

book of Acts and exhibit a literary style, doctrinal themes, and an ecclesiology that is different from Paul's other letters.[6] In the twentieth century, however, a number of scholars responded persuasively to these arguments, defending the historic position that the apostle Paul authored the Pastoral Epistles.[7]

Date and Setting

Second Timothy is the latest of all Paul's letters, written sometime shortly before his death. Eusebius claims that Paul was martyred during Nero's reign, which ended in 68, although intense persecution began in 64.[8] This probably places the letter sometime in 64–65, though some would place it as late as 67.

Paul wrote 2 Timothy during his second imprisonment in Rome (1:8). The book of Acts concludes during Paul's first imprisonment, where we find him living under house arrest for two years and with the freedom to receive visitors and even preach the gospel. Many scholars of the New Testament have persuasively argued that Paul was released after this first imprisonment and possibly traveled to Spain before being rearrested and incarcerated for a second time in Rome, an incarceration that ended in martyrdom. The gap between his first and second imprisonments was probably long enough to span at least two winters, seeing that Paul mentions such in 2 Timothy 4:21 and Titus 3:12. His second imprisonment is not recorded by Luke, for Acts does not provide us with a complete history of Paul's apostolic ministry. "It cannot be supposed that the imprisonment mentioned in Acts 28 must have ended in

---

6. See P. N. Harrison, *The Problem of the Pastorals* (London: Oxford University Press, 1921).

7. See Donald Guthrie, *The Pastoral Epistles*, Tyndale New Testament Commentaries (Downers Grove, Ill.: InterVarsity, 1990); William Hendriksen, *The Pastoral Epistles* (Grand Rapids: Baker, 1957); J. N. D. Kelly, *A Commentary on the Pastoral Epistles,* Black's New Testament Commentaries (London: A & C Black, 1963); Gordon Fee, *1 and 2 Timothy, Titus*, New International Bible Commentary (Peabody, Mass.: Hendrickson, 1988); Knight, *Pastoral Epistles*; and Mounce, *Word Biblical Commentary*, vol. 46.

8. Eusebius, *Ecclesiastical History*, 2.22.

martyrdom, for some explanation would be needed for the writer's omission to mention it. Indeed, the leniency of detention, which seems to have allowed Paul unrestricted visiting, is more suggestive of release than martyrdom."[9] The setting in 2 Timothy is completely different. Now he is in chains (1:16; 2:9), lonely (4:9–11), awaiting trial after his preliminary hearing (4:16–17), and expecting to be executed (4:6–8). He is without the comfort of books or even a cloak to stay warm (4:13). Moreover, Timothy was with Paul during his first Roman imprisonment, when he wrote the more optimistic letters of Philippians, Colossians, and Philemon. This time Timothy is absent, and Paul's tone has changed.

The city of Ephesus is the location of the church Timothy served (1 Tim. 1:3). Although modern Ephesus sits seven miles inland, the city was originally a seaport on the coast of Ionia. It was built in the tenth century BC by Greek colonists and by the time of the Roman Empire became the main city in Asia Minor. It was known for the practice of magic and sorcery, but especially for the worship of the goddess Artemis. The Temple of Artemis (completed around 550 BC) was one of the Seven Wonders of the Ancient World and formed the center of civic and religious life in Ephesus. The temple, coupled with the city's strategic harbor, made Ephesus a wealthy and cosmopolitan metropolis in the centuries leading up to the time of the apostles. It buzzed with energy and was filled with "lovers of themselves, lovers of money" (3:2) and "lovers of pleasure rather than lovers of God" (3:4). This was the context in which Timothy labored, a city that was home to the church Paul helped plant years earlier (Acts 18:18–21; 19:1–10).

Pagan religion and materialism, however, were not the only threats to the Ephesian church. When Paul penned this epistle, false teaching about Christianity was advancing aggressively in the city. In his first letter to Timothy, Paul opens with an urgent warning

9. Guthrie, *Pastoral Epistles*, 29. For more support on the second Roman imprisonment theory, see Guthrie's introduction to *Pastoral Epistles*, along with Towner, *Letters to Timothy and Titus*, 11–12.

concerning those who teach deviant doctrines contrary to the truth. His use of the present tense in the verb translated "teach no other doctrine" (1 Tim. 1:3) signifies that false teaching was not a possible future danger to the church in Ephesus but was already happening in the place where Timothy ministered. This teaching seemed to involve an incorrect (and probably quite complex) application of the Mosaic law to Christianity (1:7), incorporating speculative "fables and endless genealogies" (1:4) inspired by "deceiving spirits and doctrines of demons" (4:1). It contained a legalistic element that added to the law of God the commandments of men, such as forbidding marriage and requiring people "to abstain from foods which God created to be received with thanksgiving" (v. 3). *Heresy* is not too strong a word for this doctrine, for it caused some to "have suffered shipwreck" of the faith (1:19). Those promoting this heresy, people such as Hymenaeus, Alexander (v. 20), and Philetus (2 Tim. 2:17), were not merely deceived, but were insincere liars, "having their own conscience seared with a hot iron" (1 Tim. 4:2). They were spreading "idle babblings and contradictions of what is falsely called knowledge" (6:20).

Such was the setting in which Timothy labored. Additionally, we find the young pastor discouraged from fighting the good fight against false teaching and disheartened by Paul's incarceration. He was in need of encouragement and exhortation from his mentor and friend.

Timothy

Who was this person to whom Paul, near the end of his life, wrote this personal letter? The first time we encounter Timothy in the New Testament is in Acts 16, during Paul's second missionary journey. There, Luke describes him as "the son of a certain Jewish woman who believed, but his father was Greek," and that "he was well spoken of by the brethren who were at Lystra and Iconium" (vv. 1–2). Paul says that Timothy had been acquainted with the Scriptures from childhood (2 Tim. 3:15), probably introduced by his grandmother Lois and mother Eunice (1:5). This does not mean that Timothy knew the word of God as a Christian, but that he was raised by a Jewish mother who preserved some ties to Judaism and practiced her faith despite being married to a Gentile. Evidently, Paul was instrumental in leading Timothy to Christ, for he calls Timothy his "beloved and faithful son in the Lord" (1 Cor. 4:17), his "true son in the faith" (1 Tim. 1:2), who served him "as a son with his father" (Phil. 2:22). This is language that Paul reserves for those whom he fathered "in Christ Jesus...through the gospel" (1 Cor. 4:15; cf. Philemon 10).

Yet Timothy was more to Paul than a beloved convert; he was a faithful and trusted colleague in the ministry (Rom. 16:21). Paul mentored him (2 Tim. 3:10), took him on missionary journeys (Acts 16:3), and sent him as an apostolic representative to the churches (1 Cor. 4:17; Phil. 2:19; 1 Thess. 3:2). Timothy was with Paul on his climactic trip to Jerusalem (Acts 20:1–5) and during his first imprisonment in Rome (Phil. 1:1; Col. 1:1; Philemon 1). His name frequently appears in the opening of Paul's epistles (2 Cor. 1:1; Phil. 1:1; Col. 1:1; 1 Thess. 1:1; 2 Thess. 1:1). Among Paul's friends and colleagues, Timothy received the highest commendations. He had so proven his worth as a servant of the gospel that Paul was able to say, "I have no one like-minded [like him], who will sincerely care for your state" (Phil. 2:20). He called him "our brother and minister of God, and our fellow laborer in the gospel of Christ, to establish you and encourage you concerning your faith" (1 Thess. 3:2). Indeed, for Paul there was no one like Timothy.

Still, Timothy was not without weaknesses. He was timid by nature and prone to discouragement. Difficult tasks seemed to frighten him. So great was his trepidation that Paul found it necessary to admonish the Corinthians, "if Timothy comes, see that he may be with you without fear," and "let no one despise him" (1 Cor. 16:10–11). As the pastor of the church at Ephesus (1 Tim. 1:3), Timothy felt overwhelmed by the challenges he faced. He was afraid of suffering. His flame had burned low. Paul needed to remind him to "stir up the gift of God" (2 Tim. 1:6) and that "God has not given us a spirit of fear, but of power and of love and of a sound mind" (1:7).

Another weakness seemed to be his poor health. Timothy suffered from "frequent infirmities," warranting a medicinal remedy (1 Tim. 5:23). While we cannot be sure of the nature of this sickness, we are told that it was a recurrent problem for Timothy. It may have been a chronic illness that made it difficult for him to fulfill his regular duties of preaching, teaching, and rendering pastoral care.

There was also the matter of Timothy's age. In the Greco-Roman world, a man was still considered young until about age forty. While we do not know precisely how old Timothy was when Paul wrote this letter, we can be moderately certain that he was still in his thirties. The apostle tells him to "flee also youthful lusts" (2 Tim. 2:22). Only a few years earlier, he said, "Let no one despise your youth" (1 Tim. 4:12). This means he was probably about twenty years old when he first met the apostle in Lystra. Given his enormous responsibilities as the pastor at Ephesus (i.e., setting the church in order, standing up to false teachers, choosing elders and deacons, preaching the word), his young age was a potential liability. This young man would be accountable for carrying forth the gospel after Paul was gone.

Finally, it seems that Timothy was somewhat ashamed of Paul's imprisonment (2 Tim. 1:8). Here was an apostle of Jesus Christ suffering in prison like a common criminal. By the world's standards, he did not look successful. If he was truly the bearer of God's revelation, should not Paul be doing better than he was? Why did it seem as if God had abandoned him? Where was the power of God in Paul's life? Like most believers, Timothy still wrestled to some degree with a theology of glory. He assumed that if one is blessed by God, one should not suffer. Paul reminds him that the Christian life is patterned after Christ's life: suffering now, glory later (1:12; 2:8–9; 3:12). He urges Timothy not to be ashamed of him but rather share with him in "the sufferings for the gospel according to the power of God" (1:8; cf. 2:3; 4:5). He did not want his beloved child in the faith to abandon him as had Phygellus, Hermogenes, and Demas (1:15; 4:10).

This was Timothy: young, timid, frequently ill, and prone to discouragement. Although he was Paul's most faithful and trusted colleague, his abilities were outmatched by his responsibilities. Paul writes to him so that he might find his strength in the grace of God. Yet he also writes to us. Although Timothy is the primary recipient of this letter, he is not the only person whom Paul sought to instruct by it. The apostle wrote this letter with the broader church in mind. This is clear, at least implicitly, by Paul's using the second person plural pronoun in his benediction: "Grace be with you" (4:22).

Purpose

This letter is a farewell discourse, the last word from a spiritual father to his beloved apprentice. As noted above in the section on date and setting, the church at Ephesus was being attacked by false teaching. The gospel needed to be guarded, and its ministers needed to remain vigilant. The veteran apostle thus gives his younger colleague one final charge to "preach the word! Be ready in season and out of season" (2 Tim. 4:2), remain "watchful in all things, endure afflictions, do the work of an evangelist, [and] fulfill [his] ministry" (4:5). For Paul, this charge was necessary because he was near death (4:6–7), and the time was coming when people "will not endure sound doctrine, but according to their own desires, because they have itching ears, they will heap up for themselves teachers; and they will turn their ears away from the truth, and be turned aside to fables" (4:3–4). Some years earlier, Paul had predicted to the elders of the church at Ephesus that after his departure "savage wolves will come in among you, not sparing the flock. Also from among yourselves men will rise up, speaking perverse things, to draw away the disciples after themselves" (Acts 20:29–30). Sadly, this prediction was already being fulfilled at the time Paul wrote 2 Timothy.

The first three chapters of this letter serve as a long introduction to Paul's main charge to Timothy, which is in 4:1–5. They are filled with instruction, admonition, and encouragement as Paul urges Timothy to use his spiritual gifts for ministry (1:6–7), suffer with him for the gospel (1:8, 11–12; 2:3, 9–10; 3:12), guard the truth (1:13–14), instruct faithful men who can teach others (2:2), and remain self-disciplined (2:3–5, 15, 20–26; 3:10–14). Paul wants Timothy to heed these commands for the rest of his ministry and life.

There are many farewell discourses found in Scripture: Jacob to his sons (Genesis 49), Moses to Israel (Deuteronomy 32–33), Joshua to the elders and judges (Joshua 24), David to Solomon (1 Kings 2:1–9), and the Lord Jesus to His disciples (John 14–16). All have words of comfort and instruction for the benefit of those who will survive the one saying goodbye. What makes 2 Timothy unique is that it comes near the end of the apostolic era and highlights the transition from the extraordinary ministry of the apostles to the ordinary ministry of local pastors. Just as Pastor Timothy was called to serve as the apostle Paul's representative in the Ephesian congregation, local pastors today are called to preach, teach, and guard the same apostolic gospel.

Nearly a half century ago, John Stott wrote in the introduction to his commentary on 2 Timothy:

> The church of our day urgently needs to heed the message of the second letter of Paul to Timothy. For all around us we see Christians and churches relaxing their grasp of the gospel, fumbling it, in danger of letting it drop from their hands altogether. A new generation of young Timothys is needed, who will guard the sacred deposit of the gospel, who are determined to proclaim it and are prepared to suffer for it, and who will pass it on pure and uncorrupted to the generation which in due course will rise up to follow them.[10]

Now, some fifty years since Stott penned those words, the urgent need for a new generation of young Timothys has not diminished but only increased. Today the church desperately needs Timothys who will *guard the gospel* against false teaching, *entrust the gospel* to other faithful servants, be willing to *suffer for the gospel* like the apostle Paul, and above all, *preach the gospel* so that people will

10. John R. W. Stott, *The Message of 2 Timothy* (Downers Grove, Ill.: InterVarsity, 1973), 22.

"obtain the salvation which is in Christ Jesus with eternal glory" (2 Tim. 2:10). May God bless the church and the world by raising up a multitude of Timothys so that future generations will discover (and rediscover!) the gospel and apply it to their own times.

Outline

I. Salutation (1:1–2)

II. Encouragement, Warnings, and Instruction (1:3–3:17)

- A. Encouragement to Continue in the Ministry of the Gospel (1:3–7)
- B. Encouragement to Suffer for the Gospel (1:8–12)
- C. Encouragement to Guard the Gospel (1:13–18)
- D. Encouragement to Train Up Workmen for the Gospel (2:1–15)
- E. Warning about Those Who Oppose the Gospel (2:16–19)
- F. Encouragement to Live Consistently with the Gospel (2:20–26)
- G. Additional Warnings about Those Who Oppose the Gospel (3:1–9)
- H. Instruction about the Authority of the Gospel (3:10–17)

III. Paul's Main Charge to Timothy (4:1–8)

IV. Final Words (4:9–22)

1

Courageous for the Gospel

2 TIMOTHY 1:1–6

Paul, an apostle of Jesus Christ by the will of God, according to the promise of life which is in Christ Jesus,

To Timothy, a beloved son:

Grace, mercy, and peace from God the Father and Christ Jesus our Lord.

I thank God, whom I serve with a pure conscience, as my forefathers did, as without ceasing I remember you in my prayers night and day, greatly desiring to see you, being mindful of your tears, that I may be filled with joy, when I call to remembrance the genuine faith that is in you, which dwelt first in your grandmother Lois and your mother Eunice, and I am persuaded is in you also. Therefore I remind you to stir up the gift of God which is in you through the laying on of my hands.

Christianity is not for cowards. In a world hostile to the Christian faith, it takes courage to say that Christ is the only way to heaven. It takes courage to believe in the authority of the Bible and to be unashamed of the gospel. Courage is essential for the Christian life.

Church history is filled with inspiring accounts of people who lived and died courageously for the gospel. We think of the apostles and how they boldly proclaimed Christ and persisted in planting churches even as they faced imprisonment, torture, and death. The martyrs of the early church refused to deny the faith during the violent persecutions of Roman emperors such as Nero, Valerian, and Diocletian. We remember the Protestant Reformers during the sixteenth century who suffered for the gospel at the hands of a corrupt Roman Catholic Church. And there are millions of Christians in the modern world who courageously face persecution in places such as North Korea, China, and the Middle East.

While these accounts inspire believers, they can also cause us to reflect on our own lack of courage. Probably very few readers of this commentary are facing imprisonment or martyrdom for the faith, yet most of us are quite familiar with the sense of fear and intimidation that comes with taking a stand for Christ and His gospel. There are a thousand different situations in daily life that require courage from the Christian: the family gathering when the conversation suddenly turns to the subject of faith; the university classroom with the professor who ridicules the gospel; the lunchroom with classmates who think Christianity is an intolerant, antiquated religion; the workplace with a boss who says that he needs you to start working Sundays. Where can we find courage to live boldly for Christ? How can we overcome the crippling and debilitating sense of fear we often feel when we have the opportunity to speak up for the truth and do what is right in the eyes of God?

If you have ever felt frightened by adversaries of the gospel or discouraged by daunting circumstances, you are not alone. Fear and discouragement are common enemies to all Christians, including the original recipient of this letter, Timothy. Timid by nature, prone to illness, and faced with many challenges in the ministry, Timothy, the young pastor of the church at Ephesus, needed a lot of encouragement. He was terrified by his opponents and discouraged by his circumstances. Moreover, he was distraught over Paul's imprisonment and imminent execution.[1] Paul was his mentor and father in the faith. What would happen when the great apostle was gone? Where would he find the courage necessary to endure suffering and fulfill his calling?

---

1. For more on Timothy and the original setting of this letter, see the introduction.

Paul knew the answer. He also knew that much depended on Timothy, his "beloved child" in the faith. Soon, Paul would die. He had labored for nearly thirty years as a servant of the gospel. He was now incarcerated in Rome and facing the death penalty. Who would continue the work that the apostles had begun? Who would take the life-giving message of the gospel to the next generation? It would depend on ordinary, yet faithful men called and set apart for this task, men like Timothy. Knowing that his young protégé would face intense trials in the future, Paul wrote this epistle to encourage him. He does this not by showering him with empty compliments or shallow platitudes (something we might expect from modern-day motivational speakers), but by reminding him of his identity in Christ and giving him one final charge to fulfill his calling. That is what this short but powerful letter is all about.

Paul's charge, properly speaking, is in 4:1–5. The first three chapters of this letter serve as a long introduction to his main exhortation. They are bursting with instruction, admonition, and encouragement. Here, in the first seven verses of this letter, he describes what Timothy needs in order to serve God with courage. If Timothy was to be courageous for the gospel and finish his race, he would need to remember God's promise, receive God's grace, request God's help, and rekindle God's gift. Doing those four things regularly is essential not only for every pastor who wants to fulfill his calling but also for every Christian who wants to live courageously for Christ.

Remember God's Promise

Paul begins this epistle in a way customary of letters in the first-century Greco-Roman world. He identifies himself and states his credentials: "Paul, an apostle of Jesus Christ by the will of God" (1:1a). Even in a very personal letter such as this one, it was important for Paul to state his qualifications, for he wrote to Timothy not only as a friend and mentor but also as an apostle with the full authority given to him by the Lord Jesus. He did not appoint himself to this office; rather, he was appointed "by the will of God" (cf. Acts 9:1–31; 22:1–21). Stating this, Paul shows his intention for this letter to be received not merely as a piece of personal correspondence but also as divine revelation, which is why it is included in the canon of Scripture.

He then adds some important words to his credentials. Paul was "an apostle of Jesus Christ by the will of God, *according to the promise of life which is in Christ Jesus*" (1:1). He deliberately chose these words in order to remind Timothy of God's great promise of salvation. In one sense, he is saying, "Timothy, remember why you are serving the church at Ephesus. Remember why you must endure suffering. *It is for the gospel.* Don't be discouraged by my suffering and imprisonment. Instead, remember and focus on the message I have been preaching, which is the promise of life which is in Christ Jesus."

What exactly is "the promise of life which is in Christ Jesus"? Paul is referring to the gospel: the good news of Christ's life, death, resurrection, and ascension, which provides eternal life to all those who receive it by faith (cf. Rom. 1:16–17; 3:21–26; 1 Cor. 15:1–4; Gal. 2:16; 3:1–14). The Son of God came into this world so that we might have life. God's promise of life comes not through the law but through Christ, who fulfilled the law in our place. This promise echoes throughout the Old Testament, first in Genesis 3:15, when God said that He would bring from the woman's offspring a champion to bruise the serpent's head. This champion would reverse the curse of death that Adam had brought on the human race. Adam believed this promise and thus named his wife Eve, "because she was the mother of all living" (Gen. 3:20). The glorified, eternal life symbolized in the tree of life would come through the champion whom God had promised.

Later in redemptive history, God expanded this promise to Abraham, saying that He would make from him a great nation, giving him both an offspring and a land. Through Abraham, all the families of the earth would be blessed (Gen. 12:1–3; 15:1–21). God made these promises long before Abraham had a living son of his own. After years of waiting, Abraham fathered Isaac, from whom came Jacob and later the twelve tribes of Israel. After spending four hundred years in Egypt as slaves, the nation of Israel entered the promised land by the mighty acts of God, bringing to partial fulfillment God's promises to Abraham of a people and a land. The greater fulfillment, however, came through God's Son, Jesus Christ. It is only through Him, the last Adam, that unworthy sinners are brought to the tree of life and rescued from eternal death. It is only through Christ, the promised offspring of Abraham, that children of wrath are adopted by God and declared "Abraham's seed, and heirs according to the promise" (Gal. 3:29).

By mentioning "the promise of life which is in Christ Jesus" (1:1), Paul was reminding Timothy of what the Bible is all about: God's promise to redeem sinners through His Son. The whole purpose of Paul's apostleship was to proclaim this promise. Likewise, it was the whole purpose of Timothy's ministry. As the young pastor faced tough challenges and discouragements, he was not to lose sight of his calling to proclaim God's promise of life that is in Christ Jesus. This is the gospel that saves sinners and the gospel he was to preach.

Remembering and meditating on this promise is something all Christians are called to do. It is so easy to lose sight of the big picture and become overwhelmed with fear and discouragement from the circumstances of life in a fallen world. This is why the apostle Peter tells us, "Rest your hope fully upon the grace that is to be brought to you at the revelation of Jesus Christ" (1 Peter 1:13). Remembering "the promise of life which is in Christ Jesus" fills us with hope. God tells us that we belong to Him, body and soul, and that He has made us to enjoy Him forever. He announces to us that we have been born again to "an inheritance incorruptible and undefiled and that does not fade away, reserved in heaven for you, who are kept by the power of God through faith for salvation ready to be revealed in the last time" (1 Peter 1:4–5). God's promise of the life that is in Christ Jesus reminds us that we are pilgrims in this age. It points us to the heavenly goal that the first Adam never reached but the second Adam secured. It tells us that this life is temporary, but the best is yet to come.

Receive God's Grace

In 1:2, Paul identifies Timothy as the recipient of his epistle. This too was characteristic of letter writing in the first century. Both the sender and recipient are identified at the very beginning. This recipient, though, was Paul's "beloved son" (1:2a), for he had become Paul's son in the faith. As John Calvin put it, Paul "had begotten him in Christ; for, although this honor belongs to God alone, yet it is also transferred to ministers, whose agency he employs for regenerating us."[2] A faithful gospel ministry will have this mark. It will beget spiritual children and make disciples of Jesus Christ. Paul uses this language of the spiritual father-child relationship in other epistles to describe his bond with those whom he led to Christ and subsequently discipled. For example, writing to the church in Corinth, he says, "For though you might have ten thousand instructors in Christ, yet you do not have many fathers; for in Christ Jesus I have begotten you through the gospel" (1 Cor. 4:15). Likewise, he calls Onesimus, "my son...whom I have begotten while in my chains" (Philemon 10). Timothy was Paul's "beloved and faithful son in the Lord" (1 Cor. 4:17), his "true son in the faith" (1 Tim. 1:2), who served him "as a son with his father" (Phil. 2:22).

In the second part of 1:2, Paul gives his trademark apostolic salutation: "Grace, mercy, and peace from God the Father and Christ Jesus our Lord." This is one of those verses that we might be tempted to read without much thought, as if it is only a customary greeting and nothing else. We should resist the temptation to rush past these words, for they are inspired by the Holy Spirit and provide us with immense consolation and encouragement when we understand them. By pronouncing God's grace, mercy, and peace from God the Father and Christ Jesus our Lord, Paul does at least two important things. First, he declares God's peace treaty with Timothy through Jesus Christ, reminding him that he is the recipient of God's unconditional love and covenant faithfulness.

---

2. John Calvin, *Calvin's Commentaries*, vol. 21, *The Second Epistle to Timothy* (Grand Rapids: Baker, 1999), 184.

"Grace," the first word the apostle uses, speaks of God's complete favor freely bestowed on an undeserving sinner. Meredith Kline explains, "It is not merely the bestowal of unmerited blessings but God's blessing of man in spite of his demerits, in spite of his forfeiture of divine blessings."[3] "Mercy" is connected with grace, although slightly different. Whereas grace means receiving a good gift that one does not deserve, mercy means to not receive the just punishment that one rightly deserves.

An illustration of the difference between these two important words might be helpful. Imagine being pulled over by a highway patrolman for speeding. Let's say you were doing 80 miles per hour in a 65-mile-per-hour zone. Your heart sinks as you see blue and red lights flashing in your rearview mirror. As you bring your car to a stop on the side of the road and turn off the engine, you realize that you are in trouble. You have no valid excuse that will provide a way of escape from this unpleasant situation. You exceeded the speed limit and broke the law. Justice says that you will get what you deserve. There will be a heavy fine to pay and possibly an increase in your insurance rates, maybe even remedial traffic school. You hang your head in shame while the officer checks your driver's license, registration, and proof of insurance. But then comes a surprising change in your circumstances: the officer decides to let you off with a warning. You feel a torrent of relief as an enormous burden is suddenly lifted from you. He could have written you a speeding ticket and given you the justice you deserved, but instead he showed mercy.

Grace, however, goes a step further. Now imagine the officer, after showing you mercy by not issuing you a ticket, gave you a generous gift. "Sir, I am going to personally pay the balance you owe on this vehicle, as well as your monthly insurance premiums and annual registration for as long as you have this car. On top of that, here is $500 cash. I want you to take your family out to dinner this evening at the finest restaurant in the city." Such news not only

3. Meredith G. Kline, "Covenant Theology under Attack," *New Horizons* 15, no. 2 (1994): 3.

seems too good to be true but would be shocking and strange! We could hardly imagine an officer commissioned to enforce the law doing such a benevolent act toward someone who violated the law and deserved justice. But that's how grace works. It is shocking and strange. It is counterintuitive to the law. It moves the offender from the category of judgment to the category of favor, from demerit to merit, without him earning it at all.

The result of grace and mercy is peace, which is the third word Paul uses: "Grace, mercy, and *peace* from God the Father and Christ Jesus our Lord." Paul wanted Timothy to know that he was no longer at war with God because of his sin. Peace had been made through Jesus Christ, who, in His grace and mercy, fulfilled the law in our place through His perfect obedience and paid the debt we owed to God's justice through His substitutionary sacrifice on the cross. The apostle's salutation declared this great news to Timothy in the first century, and it is declared to every believer today: "Grace, mercy, and peace from God the Father and Christ Jesus our Lord."

There is something more subtle, though, that Paul does in his salutation. Notice the preposition he uses: "Grace, mercy, and peace *from* God the Father and Christ Jesus our Lord." In all thirteen of his letters in the New Testament, Paul begins with an apostolic greeting proclaiming God's grace to the recipient(s). He always uses some form of "Grace *to* you *from* God our Father and the Lord Jesus Christ."[4] He concludes each of his letters, however, with a benediction that uses a different preposition: "Grace be *with* you." It is always some variation of "grace *to* you" at the beginning and "grace be *with* you" at the end.[5] Paul uses these particular prepositions in

4. Paul's various salutations include "Grace to you and peace from God our Father and the Lord Jesus Christ" (Rom. 1:7b; 1 Cor. 1:3; 2 Cor. 1:2; Gal. 1:3; Eph. 1:2; Phil. 1:2; Col. 1:2b; 1 Thess. 1:1b; 2 Thess. 1:2; Philemon 3); "Grace, mercy, and peace from God our Father and Jesus Christ our Lord" (1 Tim. 1:2b); "Grace, mercy, and peace from God the Father and Christ Jesus our Lord" (2 Tim. 1:2b); and "Grace, mercy, and peace from God the Father and the Lord Jesus Christ our Savior" (Titus 1:4b).

5. Paul's benedictions are "The grace of our Lord Jesus Christ be with you" (Rom. 16:20; 1 Cor. 16:23; 1 Thess. 5:28); "The grace of the Lord Jesus Christ,

his salutations and benedictions like bookends around the bodies of each of his letters. This pattern emphasizes that God's grace to us is mediated by the Holy Spirit through the means of His word. By declaring this holy greeting, Paul was not only announcing Timothy's status as a recipient of God's grace in Christ but also highlighting the fact that this letter was nothing less than the very word of God. As he says in chapter 3 of this epistle, "All Scripture is given by inspiration of God, and is profitable for doctrine, for reproof, for correction, for instruction in righteousness, that the man of God may be complete, thoroughly equipped for every good work" (vv. 16–17; cf. 2 Peter 1:20–21). In other words, it was as if the apostle were saying in his salutation, "Timothy, I have an official message to you from God. His word comes to you as a means of His grace." Then, after declaring the word to Timothy in the four chapters of his letter, he concludes by saying in his benediction, "Now Timothy, may this grace which you have received in this letter be *with* you. May it strengthen you and uphold you as you endure suffering and fulfill your ministry."

If we want to be strengthened by the Spirit to live courageously for the gospel, we must receive the grace God provides to us in His word. The words of Scripture are not ordinary. They are God's special revelation and divine speech that bring us His grace by the power of His Spirit. This is why Paul said in his farewell to the Ephesian elders (among whom Timothy was most likely present), "So now, brethren, I commend you to God and to the word of His grace, which is able to build you up and give you an inheritance among all those who are sanctified" (Acts 20:32). "The word of His grace" is for not only our conversion (Rom. 10:17) but also our sanctification.

---

and the love of God, and the communion of the Holy Spirit be with you all" (2 Cor. 13:14); "The grace of our Lord Jesus Christ be with your spirit" (Gal. 6:18; Phil. 4:23 ESV; Philemon 25); "Grace be with all those who love our Lord Jesus Christ in sincerity" (Eph. 6:24); "Grace be with you" (Col. 4:18; 1 Tim. 6:21b); "The grace of our Lord Jesus Christ be with you all" (Phil. 4:23; 2 Thess. 3:18); "The Lord Jesus Christ be with your spirit. Grace be with you" (2 Tim. 4:22); "Grace be with you all" (Titus 3:15b).

Jesus prayed to the Father in His great High Priestly Prayer, "Sanctify them by Your truth. Your word is truth" (John 17:17). If we want to be conformed more to the image of Christ, if we want to turn from the idols of our hearts and live for God's glory, if we want the joy of the Lord to fill our lives, we need the grace God provides in His word. We never outgrow our need for this grace, which is why Paul tells Timothy (and the Holy Spirit tells every believer), "*Receive this grace!*"

Request God's Help

Verse 3 begins the body of Paul's letter. In his usual style, Paul starts with thanksgiving for the work of God's grace in the recipient of the letter. In this case, he thanks God for Timothy's sincere faith (1:5). Verses 3–5 are actually a single sentence in the original Greek. The basic structure is "I thank God" [1:3]…[for] the genuine faith that is in you" (1:5).[6] Included in this lengthy sentence are several personal comments about Paul and especially Timothy. First, Paul mentions two things about himself. He says that he serves God, "as my forefathers did" (1:3). He affirms continuity with the true faith of his Jewish ancestors, who, although living before the time of Christ, trusted God's promise as it was revealed in the Abrahamic covenant. By embracing Jesus of Nazareth as the promised Messiah, Paul served the God of Abraham. Second, he says that like his ancestors, he serves God "with a pure conscience" (1:3). In other words, Paul was seeking to live his life according to God's word and finish the ministry that he received from the Lord Jesus (4:6; cf. Acts 20:24).

Paul then tells Timothy that he is praying for him: "as without ceasing I remember you in my prayers night and day" (1:3c). The apostle was not only bringing the word to Timothy so that he could remember God's promise and receive His grace but he was

6. For more on the grammatical structure of the sentence in 1:3–5, see William D. Mounce, *Word Biblical Commentary*, vol. 46, *Pastoral Epistles* (Nashville: Thomas Nelson, 2000), 467–72; and Towner, *Letters to Timothy and Titus*, 446–55.

also praying earnestly for his apprentice. He loved this young pastor whom he had mentored over many years. He knew him well and was acquainted with members of his family. He mentions his grandmother Lois and mother Eunice, women who were known for their godliness and sincere faith (1:5). Paul ached to see his friend again: "[I am] greatly desiring to see you, being mindful of your tears, that I may be filled with joy" (1:4). He could still see Timothy's weeping face from the last time they were together. This may be a reference to the tearful farewell at Miletus (Acts 20:37) or to another occasion of which we have no record. Either way, it reveals Paul's affection for Timothy and Timothy's for Paul, a bond produced by the gospel of Jesus Christ and their shared experiences in the ministry.

We should give thanks to God for the men and women whom He has used in our lives to lead us to Christ and nurture us in the truth. The late Anglican minister, commentator, and churchman John Stott once reflected publicly on a man who was something of a Paul in his own life: "I thank God for the man who led me to Christ and for the extraordinary devotion with which he nurtured me in the early years of my Christian life. He wrote to me every week, I think, for seven years. He also prayed for me every day. I believe he still does. I can only begin to guess what I owe, under God to such a faithful friend and pastor."[7] Stott wrote that in 1973, after nearly three decades of faithful service in the Christian ministry. He would go on to serve for three more decades, completing more than sixty years as a minister who brought the gospel to countless people throughout the world through his preaching and writing. Little could his mentor have known how the Lord would use Stott when he guided him in his early years as a believer.

Is there a Paul in your life, someone mature in the faith whom the Lord has used or perhaps is still using to develop and mold you in the Christian life? Give thanks to God for him or her. You have been given a priceless gift in such a mentor. Is there a Timothy,

---

7. Stott, *Message of 2 Timothy*, 29.

someone in your life who is much younger in the faith and looks to you for guidance and encouragement as a Christian? More than likely, that tender soul sees you as a spiritual father or mother or at least a big brother or sister in Christ. Such a tremendous responsibility is understandably daunting and can fill us with fear. Yet what an awesome privilege to be used by the Lord in such a way! Pray earnestly and request God's help. Pray earnestly for that precious person as you seek by God's grace to model for that person the love of Jesus.

Paul prayed earnestly for Timothy, for he knew that very soon he would not be there for his friend. As he says near the end of this letter, "For I am already being poured out as a drink offering, and the time of my departure is at hand" (4:6). He wanted Timothy to remain faithful in the ministry, especially after his mentor had died. He wanted him to persevere in the faith and in service for the gospel. Timothy was probably not yet adequately aware of how desperately dependent he was on the grace of God. Paul knew that Timothy would need strength to "endure hardship as a good soldier of Jesus Christ" (2:3). He needed boldness to stand up to false teachers like Hymenaeus and Philetus (1:17–18). He needed wisdom to "flee also youthful lusts [and] pursue righteousness" (2:22). He needed to stay focused on his task to "preach the word," being "ready in season and out of season" (4:2). As a pastor himself, Paul knew firsthand the sort of deep discouragement Timothy was facing and would face in the future. It is a high but difficult calling to shepherd Christ's flock. It is a supernatural act of God's grace that anyone perseveres in the faith, let alone in the ministry. If Timothy was to remain faithful as a pastor and live courageously for the gospel, he would need the Lord's help. This is why Paul remembered Timothy constantly in his prayers, night and day.

Pastors need the prayers of God's people. They need our prayers to persevere in the ministry and not lose heart. Pray for your pastor, that he will serve faithfully as "a good soldier of Jesus Christ" (2:3), a self-disciplined athlete (2:5), and a "hardworking farmer" (2:6). Pray that he will rightly handle the word of truth (2:15) and that he will flee youthful passions. Pray that he will be faithful to preach the word, that he will "convince, rebuke, exhort, with all longsuffering and teaching" (4:2). Pray that he will stand up against false doctrine and not shrink back in fear and that he will not succumb to the whims of people in the congregation—yes, even your whims! Pray that he will not be swayed in his ministry by the personal agendas and itching ears of you or anyone else and that he will always be "watchful in all things, endure afflictions, do the work of an evangelist, fulfill [his] ministry" (4:5). He does not have superhero powers. He is not better than you. He is an ordinary sinner like everyone else, and he urgently needs your prayers to keep his hope anchored in Christ and remain dependent on God's grace.

Request help from God for your pastor, for others, and for yourself. If we want strength to live courageously for the gospel and unashamedly for Christ, we must not only receive the grace God provides to us in His word but also request His help through prayer. God speaks to us through His word, and we speak to Him through prayer. That is how the conversation works between God and His people. And God stands ready to receive our requests for help and give us the grace we need to persevere: "Let us therefore come boldly to the throne of grace, that we may obtain mercy and find grace to help in time of need" (Heb. 4:16).

Rekindle God's Gift

In 1:6 Paul turns from remembering Timothy in his prayers to reminding him to use the spiritual gift he had received for the work of ministry: "Therefore I remind you to stir up the gift of God which is in you through the laying on of my hands." Although the text does not specify what this gift was, we can be fairly certain that it was connected to his ordination as a minister when hands were laid on him. In his previous letter to Timothy, Paul gave a similar exhortation: "Do not neglect the gift that is in you, which was given to you by prophesy with the laying on of the hands of the eldership" (1 Tim. 4:14). These passages, along with Paul's main charge in

2 Timothy 4:2 to "preach the word," make it reasonable to conclude that Timothy was gifted by God to preach and teach.

The problem was not Timothy's gifting. God had equipped him to do the work of a minister and evangelist. When God calls a man into service, He provides him with spiritual gifts to fulfill that calling. Timothy's problem, rather, was his fear and discouragement. He had become so disheartened by both his own circumstances in Ephesus and Paul's in Rome that he apparently began to lose motivation. He seems also to have grown somewhat embarrassed by Paul's imprisonment (1:8). Many of Paul's colleagues and supporters forsook him when he was rearrested and put in chains (1:15). Timothy too seemed to be wrestling with this difficulty. If Paul was commissioned by the Lord Jesus Christ, to whom had been given all authority in heaven and on earth, why was he incarcerated (again) and now facing execution? Paul's life was so full of hardships that he did not appear to have God's blessing. If he was blessed by God and a true apostle, why did he suffer so much? Shouldn't he be doing better? Shouldn't his mission be more successful? This seems to be behind much of Timothy's discouragement and fear. Consequently, he had become so immobilized with timidity and disillusionment that his zeal was burning at a very low flame, causing him to neglect the gift God had given him.

Paul gives his beloved colleague a gentle wake-up call: "Therefore I remind you to stir up the gift of God which is in you through the laying on of my hands. For God has not given us a spirit of fear, but of power and of love and of a sound mind" (1:6–7). It seems that Timothy (like those who had turned away from Paul) was assuming the common theology of glory that comes so naturally to us all. A theology of glory says that if God is powerfully at work in our lives, He should deliver us from suffering. When we suffer, we tend to assume that we are somehow lacking God's power and blessing. This naturally leads to fear and discouragement. Paul tells us that such thinking is totally contrary to the gospel and the way the Spirit operates in Christ's people. God's power is made manifest in our suffering and weakness. As the Lord said to Paul, "My grace is sufficient for you, for My strength is made perfect in weakness" (2 Cor. 12:9). Martin Luther called this a theology of the cross, which is contrary to a theology of glory. A theology of the cross understands that the Christian life is patterned after the life of our Lord. It is suffering now, glory later.

We too need this reminding. If you are suffering, do not assume that God has abandoned you. If you are discouraged and facing fearful circumstances, do not conclude that God is not blessing you. Do not think that God's mission has failed. Understand that God is operating in His standard way. He has supplied you with His Spirit, who equips you with all you need as He conforms you more to the image of Christ. First comes suffering, then comes glory. That was the pattern of our Lord's life, and it will be the pattern of our lives. It is through suffering for the gospel, through suffering the ridicule of the world, through hardships and difficulties that God is fulfilling His mission, and He does it according to His perfect timing and infinite wisdom.

In the meantime, rekindle the gift God has given you. Fan it into flame! Remember God's promise, "the promise of the life that is in Christ Jesus." Receive His grace that is provided to you abundantly in His word. Request His help in prayer. God has not given you a spirit of fear, Christian.

2

A Spirit of Power, Love, and Self-Control

2 TIMOTHY 1:7

For God has not given us a spirit of fear, but of power and of love and of a sound mind.

On April 16, 1521, Martin Luther arrived in the city of Worms to appear before the imperial court of the Holy Roman Empire. The previous year, Pope Leo X issued a papal bull against the German monk for his writings. Now Luther was summoned before the emperor Charles V and the electors, princes, and nobility of the empire to renounce his views. The following day, in the presence of the whole court, he was asked two simple questions: "Do you, Martin Luther, recognize the books published under your name as your own? Are you prepared to recant what you have written in these books?"[1] To the first question, Luther answered yes. To the second, though, he wavered. Offering an answer to this question was more than he could handle at that moment. He realized that if he did not recant, there was a very good possibility that he would be condemned as a heretic, taken to Rome, and burned at the stake. Feeling in over his head, he asked for some time to think about how he should answer. The court granted him one day.

We can imagine the sort of fear that Luther must have felt as he mulled over his options that night. The Reformation was on the

1. As quoted in Heiko Oberman, *Luther: Man between God and the Devil* (New Haven, Conn.: Yale University Press, 1982), 38.

line, but so was his life. Where would he find the strength to do what was right and speak the truth in the face of harm?

Fear can be crippling. It can paralyze us when we ought to act and silence us when we ought to speak. This is one of the chief reasons why the apostle Paul near the end of his life wrote this very personal letter to Timothy. Like Luther at the Diet of Worms, Timothy faced a situation in the church of Ephesus that caused him to feel that he was in over his head. Persuasive false teachers were launching attacks on the gospel. Some in the church were questioning his authority as a pastor. He was discouraged and probably embarrassed about Paul's imprisonment and declining reputation. He needed to stand up for the truth and faithfully preach the word of God, but he was afraid of suffering. His flame was burning low. Paul found it urgent to remind this young pastor whom he had mentored to fan into flame the gift of God (2 Tim. 1:6) and that "God has not given us a spirit of fear, but of power and of love and of a sound mind" (1:7).

We need that reminder too. Our circumstances can sometimes make us feel that we are in over our head. At times it is quite certain that God has given us far more than we can handle. But it is also true that the Holy Spirit has equipped us in a threefold way so that we can fulfill our callings and persevere in the faith, even in the face of fear. Before we move on to the next section in 2 Timothy, we should pause and meditate on this important verse: "God has not given us a spirit of fear, but of power and of love and of a sound mind." In one sense, this verse represents the entire focus of Paul's letter.

A Spirit Not of Fear

It is important to understand the kind of fear of which Paul speaks in this verse, for the Bible talks about fear in different ways. There is a kind of fear that believers are called to pursue—namely, the fear of the Lord. The book of Proverbs tells us that "the fear of the LORD is the beginning of wisdom" (9:10) and "a fountain of life" (14:27). Psalm 19:9 says that "the fear of the LORD is clean, enduring forever." The author of Ecclesiastes sums up his whole book by reminding us to "fear God and keep His commandments, for this is man's all" (12:13). The fear of the Lord is one of the central themes in the Scriptures, for it expresses the way in which humans were designed to live in relationship to their Creator. To fear the Lord is to revere, respect, honor, and love Him. It means recognizing that God has the first priority in everything and that we exist for His glory and good pleasure.

But the Bible also speaks of a fear that is sinful. When we fear anything more than we fear God, we are guilty of an idolatrous and unholy fear. The Lord warned Israel that to fear man rather than God is essentially to forget that God is sovereign:

> I, even I, am He who comforts you.
> Who are you that you should be afraid
> Of a man who will die,
> And of the son of a man who will be made like grass?
> And you forget the LORD your Maker,
> Who stretched out the heavens
> And laid the foundations of the earth. (Isa. 51:12–13a)

Likewise, Jesus said, "Do not fear those who kill the body but cannot kill the soul. But rather fear Him who is able to destroy both soul and body in hell" (Matt. 10:28).

The fear of man is not limited to being afraid of people who might cause us bodily harm. More often than not, we demonstrate our fear of man by fearing others' disapproval. Instead of finding our identity and value in God, where it properly lies, we look for it in the opinion of others. We want people to think highly of us, so we do all we can to protect our reputation. We are afraid of failing, so we procrastinate. We are petrified of saying something that others might consider to be stupid, so we say nothing. We are fearful of looking foolish in front of others, so we hesitate on taking action. We dread being discovered as a fraud and a fake, so we put on our best act and pretend to have it all together. Our desire for approval and fear of disapproval can be so strong at times that they lead us into an exhausting life full of worry, disappointment, and frustration. This is why Proverbs tells us that "the fear of man brings a snare, but whoever trusts in the LORD shall be safe" (29:25).

The fear of which Paul speaks in 1:7 is not the fear of the Lord, but the fear of man. In fact, the word that Paul uses for fear (*deilias*), which is used only this one time in the entire New Testament, means "cowardice and fearfulness that causes a person to compromise his principles when it becomes risky to hold them." Unlike the more common word for fear found in the New Testament (*phobos*), this word is used only in a negative sense. It is never used to describe the fear of the Lord. In other words, Paul emphasizes to Timothy that the fear of man is not from God, for "God has not given us a spirit of fear." The emphatic position of "not" (*ou*) emphasizes this fact.

Most English translations render the word "spirit" (*pneuma*) in 1:7 with a lowercase *s* rather than with a capital, which would indicate the Holy Spirit. This seems to be the more natural reading of the text and corresponds to other places in his letters where Paul uses the word *spirit* to describe a person's attitude or disposition.[2] While this interpretation may be accurate, it is nevertheless important that we recognize the role of the Holy Spirit forming this new spirit in us. The Holy Spirit Himself is a gift to all believers and the down payment of their future inheritance (John 7:39; 14:16–17; Acts 2:38; 10:45; Gal. 3:14; Eph. 1:13–14). He regenerates them, indwells them, and equips them with qualities that are essential for serving God and their neighbor—namely, power, love, and self-control.[3] These graces

---

2. See the following: "spirit of bondage" (Rom. 8:15); "spirit of stupor" (Rom. 11:8); "spirit of gentleness" (1 Cor. 4:21; Gal. 6:1); "no rest in my spirit" (2 Cor. 2:13); "spirit of faith" (2 Cor. 4:13); "his spirit has been refreshed by you all" (2 Cor. 7:13); and "stand fast in one spirit" (Phil. 1:27). As William Mounce notes, Paul's use of the word "spirit" in these references "is not quite the same as the use of *pneuma* that designates the human spirit from the body, but it is related." See *Word Biblical Commentary*, vol. 46, 477.

3. There has been a long-standing debate among New Testament scholars on whether Paul intended in 1:7 to write about the Holy Spirit or the spirit that the Holy Spirit formed in Timothy and likewise in all believers. Most conclude that there is an undeniable connection between the two. Perhaps Patrick Fairbairn said it best in his comments on this passage: "By *spirit* here may be understood either God's Spirit working in a certain manner in us, or our own spirit as wrought upon

are a small manifestation of what the Spirit will give to believers in full measure at the resurrection on the last day.

In one sense, what Paul says to Timothy in 1:7 is an echo of what he wrote years earlier in Romans 8:15: "For you did not receive the spirit of bondage again to fear, but you received the Spirit of adoption by whom we cry out, 'Abba, Father.'" Paul applies this text to Timothy in his present situation. He wants his young colleague to be assured that the Holy Spirit whom he had received was producing in him a spirit of power, love, and self-control. Although Timothy faced many distressing challenges in the church at Ephesus, he did not need to live as a slave to his fears, for God had adopted him through the finished work of His Son and set him free. Fear, therefore, no longer defined Timothy as a person. He had received a new identity in Christ.

The same is true of you, Christian. If you are in Christ, you have been set free. You are free from the power of sin (John 8:34–36; Rom. 6:18, 22–23), free from the condemnation of the law (Rom. 8:1–2; Gal. 5:1), and free from the tyranny of fear. This is your new identity in Christ.

What are those things in life that make you feel afraid and anxious? Do you dread the uncertainty of the future? Are you nervous about your circumstances taking a turn for the worse? Do you fear losing the people or possessions that are most important to you? Are you living as if God were not in control of things? If so, remember that your identity is in Christ. Remember who you are. Your fears, regardless of how strong they may feel, do not define you. The living God has become your heavenly Father. He has adopted you in Christ and given you His Spirit, not a spirit of fear. Because of the finished work of Christ, God is for you, not against you. He is sovereign over all things and will not allow anything to happen to you apart from His will. We can say with confidence with Heidelberg

and formed by God; practically, it comes much to the same thing, since either way the gift is of God, obtained by direct fellowship with His Spirit." *A Commentary on 1 & 2 Timothy and Titus* (1874; repr., Edinburgh: Banner of Truth, 2002), 315.

Catechism 26 that God "is for the sake of Christ, His Son, my God and my Father, in whom I so trust as to have no doubt that He will provide me with all things necessary for body and soul; and further, that whatever evil He sends upon me in this troubled life, He will turn to my good; for He is able to do it, being Almighty God, and willing also, being a faithful Father."

Perhaps it is not the uncertainty of the future that you fear but people and their disapproval. Are you afraid of being hurt by people? Do you fear rejection? Do you fear failure? Are you terrified of embarrassment and shame? Are you frightened to lose the high opinion of others? You do not need to be governed by these fears. The Son of God came into this world and took on Himself our sin, shame, failure, and disgrace. We are now clothed in His righteousness and perfection. This is our true identity. We can say boldly with the psalmist,

> The LORD is on my side;
> I will not fear.
> What can man do to me? (Ps. 118:6; cf. Heb. 13:6)

A Spirit of Power

An old adage about courage says that "courage is not the absence of fear, but the willingness to do what is right even when you are terrified." A pithier version attributed to John Wayne goes, "Courage is being scared to death and saddling up anyway." Such sayings are fine as far as they go, but they fail to tell us where to find courage. Ultimately, they suggest that courage is something that we must conjure up in our own strength.

Similarly, there is a popular slogan in American Christianity that "God will never give you more than you can handle." This is not a saying with which the apostle Paul would have agreed.[4] Over the

4. The saying "God will never give you more than you can handle" is usually a misapplication of 1 Corinthians 10:13, which says, "No temptation has overtaken you except such as is common to man; but God is faithful, who will not allow you to be tempted beyond what you are able, but with the temptation will also make the way of escape, that you may be able to bear it." This passage, however, speaks

course of his thirty-year ministry, Paul found the very opposite to be true. He was often in over his head. There were times when he was overwhelmed by extreme hardship and affliction (2 Cor. 11:24–28). More than once he pled with the Lord to lighten the load of his suffering because it was more than he could bear (12:7–8). Paul persevered through these fiery trials not because he was strong enough to handle them or because he fabricated thc strength to "saddle up" anyway but because he trusted in God's sufficient grace. Sometimes God does give us more than we can handle. But He also gives us the grace we need in order to endure, and His grace is always sufficient (vv. 9–10).

This is the promise that Paul sought to impress on Timothy as he felt weak and defeated by his fears. The apostle did not offer Timothy empty platitudes about courage and self-sufficiency. Instead, after telling him that God did not give us a spirit of fear, he proceeded to name a triad of graces with which the Holy Spirit has equipped us. The first of these is power: "God has not given us a spirit of fear, but of power." The Greek word that Paul uses for power is *dunamis*. Throughout the New Testament, this word is often associated with the third person of the Holy Trinity (Luke 4:14; Acts 1:8; Rom. 15:13, 19; Eph. 3:16). God the Spirit supplies power to believers as He indwells them so that they will be strengthened "for all patience and longsuffering with joy" (Col. 1:11). Fear is disabling, but power is enabling. God gives believers what they need so that they can fulfill their callings. This strength comes not from ourselves, but from "the grace that is in Christ Jesus" (2 Tim. 2:1).

We usually feel our weakest when our fears are strongest. But God tells us that our weakness and lack of ability are not fatal to the tasks to which He has called us. They are not even defects or hindrances. In reality, our weakness is essential to our callings, for it is in our weakness that God's power is made perfect. He makes

about the temptation to sin, not suffering in general. It is a promise that God will not allow believers to be tempted beyond what they are able to bear, not that God will never give believers "more than they can handle."

His power available to us by the Holy Spirit not to make us look self-sufficient to the world but to display His glory in weak and imperfect people. Whatever your circumstances may be right now, Jesus says to you, "My grace is sufficient for you, for My strength is made perfect in weakness" (2 Cor. 12:9).

A Spirit of Love

Just as the Holy Spirit supplies believers with power, He also supplies them with love (*agape*). Love is a powerful antidote to fear. As John says in his first epistle, "There is no fear in love; but perfect love casts out fear" (4:18). Perfect love is found in Jesus Christ, who loved us and gave himself for us (Gal. 2:20). We did nothing to merit this love, for He loved us while we were still sinners and His enemies (Rom. 5:8–10). Nothing soothes our troubled heart more than to be reassured that we are the recipients of God's eternal love in Christ and that He will "preserve [us] for His heavenly kingdom" (2 Tim. 4:18).

Paul reminds Timothy that it is through the Spirit that God pours His love into our hearts (Rom. 5:5) and makes it manifest in our lives toward our neighbor (Gal. 5:22; cf. Col. 1:8). As the early church father John Chrysostom put it, "For the Spirit that makes us cry, 'Abba, Father,' inspires us with love both toward him and toward our neighbor, that we may love one another. For love arises from power and not from fearing."[5] The Spirit who supplies us with power also supplies us with love so that we can serve others and not shrink back in fear. Love does not seek its own good but the good of others, even at the expense of what is dear to us. It aims for the glory of God, not the glory of self. It is love produced by the Holy Spirit that caused Paul to write, "I endure all things for the sake of the elect, that they also may obtain the salvation which is in Christ Jesus with eternal glory" (2 Tim. 2:10). It is love for God and people

---

5. John Chrysostom, *Homilies on 2 Timothy*, in *Ancient Christian Commentary on Scripture*, ed. Thomas C. Oden, New Testament vol. 9 (Downers Grove, Ill.: InterVarsity, 2000), 232.

that moved Paul to say, "But none of these things move me; nor do I count my life dear to myself, so that I may finish my race with joy, and the ministry which I received from the Lord Jesus, to testify to the gospel of the grace of God" (Acts 20:24).

Fear turns us inward, focusing our attention on our own benefit, well-being, and reputation. Love instead turns us toward our neighbors and their benefit and well-being. Fear asks, "What will I lose? How will I be hurt? What if I fail? What's going to happen to me?" But love asks, "How can I give? How can I help? What can I do for others?" God has given us a spirit not of fear but of love.

A Spirit of Self-Control

God supplies us with a third quality for overcoming fear. Along with power and love, the Spirit provides believers with self-control. The Greek word that Paul uses for "a sound mind" (*sophronismos*) occurs only this once in the New Testament, and there are a number of English words that capture its meaning from different perspectives: self-control, self-discipline, sobriety, sound-mindedness, and moderation all work to some degree. The word conveys the idea of remaining calm in a difficult situation and avoiding reckless behavior by controlling actions and thoughts. In this context, Paul applies it to Timothy's situation of facing frightening circumstances and the need for clarity of thought—as Philip Towner put it, "to trust in the invisible God despite the threats of very visible opponents."[6] Patrick Fairbairn said of this quality that it "shows itself in a capacity to check what, either by corrupt motions from within, or by threats and allurements from without, would lead us into foolish and perverse ways: it is the power of authoritative control and wise restraint, which if we but have in sufficient measure, we shall not weakly bend to adverse circumstances, but make these bend to us."[7]

As he wrote to Timothy from a Roman prison, the apostle Paul demonstrated how this Spirit-wrought self-control operates. Paul

6. Towner, *Letters to Timothy and Titus*, 462.

7. Fairbairn, *Commentary on 1 & 2 Timothy and Titus*, 315–16.

was cold, lonely, and facing execution. His reputation among many had deteriorated. Some had abandoned him. Yet he labored faithfully for the gospel until the very end. He says, "For I am already being poured out as a drink offering, and the time of my departure is at hand. I have fought the good fight, I have finished the race, I have kept the faith" (2 Tim. 4:6–7). How could he be so self-controlled in such a dire situation? How did he maintain his composure and confidence, especially when so many had deserted him? The answer is that he, like all believers, was equipped by the Spirit of God who supernaturally works in us a spirit of self-control.

This triple grace of power, love, and self-control is a gift purchased for us by the Lord Jesus Christ. The Son of God came into this world to "release those who through fear of death were all their lifetime subject to bondage" (Heb. 2:15). Jesus accomplished our redemption through His perfect obedience to the Father, even when His soul was disturbed and troubled. Contemplating the cross as He came into Jerusalem to die for our sins, He said, "Now My soul is troubled, and what shall I say? 'Father, save Me from this hour'? But for this purpose I came to this hour. Father, glorify Your name" (John 12:27–28). His love for us and for the Father's glory caused Him to overcome His fears of facing the wrath of God as our sins were laid on Him. Praying in the garden of Gethsemane on the night before He was crucified, He cried out in distress, "Father, if it is Your will, take this cup away from Me." Yet, because of His love for the Father and for those He came to save, He submitted himself to the Father's will and said, "Nevertheless not My will, but Yours, be done" (Luke 22:42). He maintained self-control as He was "despised and rejected by men, a Man of sorrows and acquainted with grief" (Isa. 53:3). He bore the weight of our guilt as "He was wounded for our transgressions [and]...bruised for our iniquities" (v. 5). His life, death, and resurrection have secured for us the gift of the Spirit, who works in our hearts a spirit of power, love, and self-control.

The Holy Spirit has been given to us not to remove every form of suffering in this life but to conform us to the image of Christ (cf. Rom. 8:15–17). He is the down payment of the full inheritance we will receive in glory (Eph. 1:13–14). God's Spirit gives us *power* to persevere in this life, even in the midst of the most difficult trials and hardships, providing us with the grace we need to go through them. He provides us with *love*, the first evidence of the fruit of the Spirit (Gal. 5:22), so that we can use our gifts sincerely not for our personal gain or advancement but for the genuine benefit of others. He strengthens us with *self-control* so that we can serve others with self-discipline in regard to our thoughts and behavior, despite the discouragement of suffering or the threat of opponents.

Maybe you feel a lot like Timothy. Maybe you fear man far more than you should. Maybe you are terrified of failing and looking bad in front of others. Remember that in Christ God has treated you with grace and mercy. In Christ He is not against you but for you. In Christ you have a new identity, an identity that does not depend on the opinion of others or on your circumstances. You can say with the psalmist,

> The LORD is on my side;
> I will not fear.
> What can man do to me? (Ps. 118:6)

This is the same Spirit who empowered Luther during his frightening predicament at the Diet of Worms. Luther submitted his answer to the court on the following day. By the grace of God, he was able to say,

> Some of my books are neither sharp nor polemical. They deal with nothing but faith and the Christian life in accordance with the gospel. Even my opponents will be able to find nothing objectionable in them. Other writings are directed against the papacy, which is ruining the church, weighing down the human conscience and oppressing the empire. If I were to recant these, then, I would be doing nothing but strengthening tyranny.... Unless I am convinced by the testimony of the Holy Scriptures or by evident reason—for I can believe neither pope nor councils alone, as it is clear that they have erred repeatedly and contradicted themselves—I consider myself to

> be convicted by the testimony of the Holy Scripture, which is my basis. My conscience is captive to the Word of God. Thus, I cannot and will not recant, because acting against one's conscience is neither safe nor sound. Here I stand. God help me. Amen.[8]

The same Spirit who strengthened Luther at Worms and Timothy at Ephesus is at work in you today, for He has given you the same thing He gave those men, a spirit not of fear but of power, love, and self-control.

---

8. As quoted in Oberman, *Luther: Man between God and the Devil*, 38–39.

3

A Gospel Worth Suffering For

2 TIMOTHY 1:8–12

Therefore do not be ashamed of the testimony of our Lord, nor of me His prisoner, but share with me in the sufferings for the gospel according to the power of God, who has saved us and called us with a holy calling, not according to our works, but according to His own purpose and grace which was given to us in Christ Jesus before time began, but has now been revealed by the appearing of our Savior Jesus Christ, who has abolished death and brought life and immortality to light through the gospel, to which I was appointed a preacher, an apostle, and a teacher of the Gentiles. For this reason I also suffer these things; nevertheless I am not ashamed, for I know whom I have believed and am persuaded that He is able to keep what I have committed to Him until that Day.

On November 2, 1561, Philip II of Spain, a staunch Roman Catholic king and sworn enemy of the Reformation, was lodging at a castle in the French-speaking city of Tournai. That day, the gatekeeper found a package that had been thrown over the castle wall containing a letter addressed to the king and a copy of a newly drafted Protestant confession of faith written primarily by Guido de Brés, a local Reformed pastor who had studied under John Calvin. The letter informed the king that Protestants in his realm wished to meet with him in person and justly plead their cause but that his violent persecution of them made such a meeting impossible. It also explained that Protestants were not lawbreakers and revolutionaries, as the king had claimed, but were willing and ready to obey him in all lawful matters. The point on which they could not submit to the king, however, was the Christian faith as summarized in their confession. Rather than deny the gospel of Jesus Christ, they said, "[we would] suffer our backs to be beaten, our tongues to be cut, our mouths to be gagged and our whole bodies to be burnt, for we know that he who would follow Christ must take up his cross and deny himself."[1] Their confession became known as the Belgic Confession, one of the most loved and widely known confessions of the sixteenth-century Protestant Reformation. It is still in use to this day by Reformed churches throughout the world.

At the hand of Philip II, thousands of Protestants, including de Brés himself, did seal the Belgic Confession with their own blood. Some historians estimate the number of those martyrs to be around one hundred thousand. They were willing to suffer for the gospel because they believed that the gospel was worth suffering for.

What are you willing to suffer for? For what truth or cause would you be willing to die if necessary? We can probably think of many things. Countless mothers, for the sake of their children, are willing to suffer the pain of childbirth along with innumerable discomforts and sacrifices in the years of their child's upbringing. Combat veterans have proved their willingness to suffer the horrors of battle for their country and fellow soldiers. People with cancer are often willing to suffer the ravages of chemotherapy and radiation treatment in order to extend their lives. There are many things in life that human beings believe are worthy of suffering for: family, friends, health, success. But ask yourself this: Is there anything more worthy of our suffering than the gospel of Jesus Christ? Only the gospel can meet humanity's greatest need by cleansing the conscience of guilt, providing the righteousness of Christ, and promising unworthy sinners eternal life.

The apostle Paul wanted to impress on Timothy the worthiness of suffering for the gospel. As he served the church at Ephesus as their minister, Timothy needed to face his fears and stand up to

1. As quoted in Daniel R. Hyde, *With Heart and Mouth: An Exposition of the Belgic Confession* (Grandville, MI: Reformed Fellowship, 2008), 16.

those who opposed the gospel. He would need to carry the baton after Paul's death. But in order to do that, he would also need to be convinced that the gospel is worth suffering for. Here in 2 Timothy 1:8–12, Paul pens one of the most magnificent statements about the gospel, compressing several immense doctrines into one long sentence in Greek. Like Timothy, we too can be encouraged from this passage and see how the gospel is worth suffering for.

Suffering or Shame?

After reminding Timothy that God did not give him "a spirit of fear, but of power and of love and of a sound mind" (1:7), Paul tells his younger cohort that his ministry is to be marked by suffering rather than shame. He exhorts him to be unashamed of the gospel: "Therefore do not be ashamed of the testimony of our Lord" (1:8a). The phrase "the testimony of our Lord" is another way of saying "the gospel." The gospel is the good news, the testimony about the life, death, and resurrection of Jesus Christ and what His work accomplishes for us (1 Cor. 15:1–6). It is the testimony of which the apostles themselves were eyewitnesses.

As glorious as this good news is, though, the fear of man can tempt us to feel ashamed of it. Like Peter when he denied our Lord (Luke 22:54–62), we may find ourselves in situations where we nervously try to blend in and not draw any attention to the fact that we are followers of Christ. We might avoid conversations about religion for fear of embarrassment. We may feel uncomfortable if certain people discover that we believe in the authority of the Bible and doctrines like creation, original sin, the incarnation, and the resurrection. Timothy also felt these pressures. In his day, the message of Christ crucified was "to the Jews a stumbling block and to the Greeks foolishness" (1 Cor. 1:23). Moreover, there was a false teaching circulating in Ephesus that incorporated speculative "fables and endless genealogies" (1 Tim. 1:4) and included the claim that "the resurrection is already past" (2 Tim. 2:17–18). Standing up for the truth of the gospel was not a popular position to take in society.

Paul exhorts Timothy not to succumb to his fears but instead to remain unashamed of "the testimony of our Lord."

The fear of man can also make us feel ashamed to be associated with Christ's people. Paul warns Timothy about this too: "Therefore do not be ashamed of the testimony of our Lord, *nor of me His prisoner*" (1:8). It seems that when Paul was rearrested and imprisoned for a second time in Rome, some of his former friends and colleagues disowned him (1:15; 4:10). They may have viewed his incarceration as evidence that Paul was not blessed by God and therefore not a true apostle. In the eyes of the world, Paul was the prisoner of Caesar and an enemy of Rome. In reality, however, he was the Lord's prisoner and a servant of the kingdom of God.[2] He was held in a Roman prison for Christ's sake. Although his suffering may have appeared unattractive to many, he was undergoing this trial by the Lord's design. The pattern to which believers are called to conform is the pattern of Christ Himself: suffering now, glory later (Acts 14:22; Rom. 8:17; Phil. 3:10; 2 Tim. 2:12). Knowing this, Paul presses Timothy not to follow the example of those who forsook him. Just as Timothy must not be ashamed of the Lord, he must not be ashamed of the Lord's apostle either. We cannot be ashamed of one without being ashamed of the other.

Timothy had therefore two options: suffering or shame. Would he cower in fear and be ashamed of the gospel, or would he be willing to suffer for it? Paul exhorts Timothy to do the latter. Yet he does so with the encouragement that he has been equipped for this task: "Share with me in the sufferings for the gospel according to the power of God" (1:8b). The power with which the Holy Spirit supplied Timothy (1:7) would strengthen him to persevere while suffering for the gospel.

This choice between suffering and shame, though, was not Timothy's alone. The same choice belongs to us. Every Christian

---

2. See Ephesians 3:1 where Paul, writing from a prison cell during his first Roman incarceration, calls himself "the prisoner of Christ Jesus for you Gentiles"; and 4:1, where he says he is "the prisoner of the Lord." He makes a similar reference in Philemon 9.

is called to be a witness to Christ before the world. The question is this: Will we cower in our fear of man and be ashamed of the gospel, or are we willing to suffer for it? The fact is that, as Paul says later in his letter, "all who desire to live godly in Christ Jesus will suffer persecution" (3:12). Likewise, Jesus said to His disciples, "'A servant is not greater than his master.' If they persecuted Me, they will also persecute you" (John 15:20). We need not fear suffering, however, for God has given us a spirit not of fear but of power. He has equipped us to endure suffering and has promised to award us with the crown of righteousness on the last day (2 Tim. 4:8).

To help Timothy (and us) remain unashamed of the gospel, Paul explains in 1:9–10 why the gospel is worth suffering for. In this carefully constructed passage, the apostle touches on five magnificent aspects of our salvation in Christ that the gospel announces to us: *election*, *calling*, *justification*, *sanctification*, and *glorification*. Although Paul does not put them in this particular order as he does elsewhere in his writings (see Rom. 8:29–30), it may be helpful for us to consider them in this logical sequence, as all five of these doctrines are represented in these two verses. We typically refer to this arrangement as the *ordo salutis* (order of salvation) or the golden chain of salvation. To use a different metaphor, these five doctrines are like different cuts on the same jewel that cause it to shine gloriously and display its beauty more brilliantly.

The Gospel Includes Our Election

Paul explains to Timothy the basis for his imperative in 1:8 by stating a majestic indicative in 1:9: God "has saved us and called us with a holy calling, not according to our works, but according to His own purpose and grace which was given to us in Christ Jesus before time began." He uses a participle in the aorist tense—"who has saved us"—to emphasize that God's gracious act is a finished act. Paul helps Timothy see afresh the glory of the gospel by reminding him that his salvation began not with his decision to trust in Christ but with God's gracious act before the foundation of the world.

It is not uncommon to hear Christians speak about their salvation as happening at the time of their conversion. "When were you saved?" the question is sometimes asked. "I got saved when I was in my early twenties," and so on. But *salvation* in the biblical sense of the term means far more than the time of our conversion. It encompasses the whole purpose of God in redeeming a people for Himself and includes His sovereign act of electing these people for salvation "before time began." In order to trace our salvation back to its original source, we must go back in time to a past eternity.

The doctrine of election teaches, as article 16 of the Belgic Confession summarizes, that God "is merciful in withdrawing and saving from perdition those whom he, in his eternal and unchangeable counsel, has elected and chosen in Jesus Christ our Lord by his pure goodness, without any consideration of their works." God's election of sinners to salvation was not based on any condition or requirement fulfilled by those whom He chose to save but solely "according to His own purpose and grace" (1:9; cf. Rom. 8:29–30; 9:10–24; Eph. 1:4–6, 11; Col. 3:12).

It is significant that Paul specifies that before the ages began this grace was given to us *in Christ Jesus*. This is a reference to the covenant of redemption, an agreement between the Father and the Son before the foundation of the world to bring sinners to glory. The covenant of redemption is essentially God's blueprint for our salvation. Just as a house, ship, or other structure begins with a plan of meticulous engineering and technical design, so also did our redemption originate on the drafting table of God. Before the ages began, a plan was already in place to send the Son as the second Adam to remedy the disastrous results of the first Adam's failure to fulfill the covenant of works in the garden of Eden and bring humankind to glory. The covenant of redemption was not a "plan B" to fix the mess Adam made but the original design for the work of Christ and the plan of redemption. Out of a fallen and condemned mass of humanity, the Father chose sinners who were no more deserving or qualified to be saved than those whom He did not choose. He chose them in Christ unconditionally and according to His own purpose. The

Father gave these elect sinners to the Son and sent Him into this world to accomplish the work of their redemption.[3]

This is good news for all who put their trust in Jesus Christ. The source of our salvation is not found in ourselves, but in God. What joy and comfort this should bring to our hearts! "The doctrine of election is never introduced in Scripture either to arouse or baffle our carnal curiosity," said John Stott, "but always for a practical purpose. On the one hand, it engenders deep humility and gratitude, for it excludes all boasting. On the other, it brings both peace and assurance, for nothing can quiet our fears for our own stability like the knowledge that our safety depends ultimately not on ourselves but on God's own purpose of grace."[4]

The Gospel Includes Our Calling

The next cut on the jewel of salvation is our calling: God, "who has saved us and called us" (1:9). Paul sets these two participles side by side to emphasize the work of the Holy Spirit in our conversion, effectually calling us out of darkness and into light. God not only elected us to salvation before the ages began but He also ensured that at some point in our lives we would put our trust in Jesus Christ alone for salvation. As our Lord Himself said, "All that the Father gives Me will come to Me, and the one who comes to Me I will by no means cast out" (John 6:37).

Without the gracious and powerful work of the Holy Spirit, this would be impossible, for the radical corruption of the human heart caused by the fall of Adam left us incapable of coming to

---

3. Other passages that refer to Christ receiving the elect from the Father or coming to accomplish the work the Father gave Him to do include John 4:34; 5:30, 36, 43; 6:37–40; 10:18; 12:49; 14:31; 15:10; 17:1–5; 19:30. Likewise, Old Testament passages such as Psalm 40:6–8; Psalm 110; Isaiah 53; and Zechariah 6:12–13 all reveal a covenantal relationship of obedience and reward between the Father and the Son, thus forming the backdrop of the covenant of redemption. For more on the covenant of redemption, see Michael G. Brown and Zach Keele, *Sacred Bond: Exploring Covenant Theology* (Grand Rapids: Reformed Fellowship, 2012).

4. Stott, *Message of 2 Timothy*, 36.

Jesus on our own. Adam was our federal representative in the garden, which means that when he rebelled against God, the whole human race inherited guilt and pollution (Rom. 5:12, 18–19). As some of the Puritans used to say, "In Adam's fall, sinned we all." Each of us is conceived and born in iniquity (Ps. 51:5). The prophet Jeremiah says,

> The heart is deceitful above all things,
> And desperately wicked;
> Who can know it? (Jer. 17:9)

In Ephesians 2:1–3, Paul describes our condition before the Holy Spirit effectually called us to Christ: "And you He made alive, who were dead in trespasses and sins, in which you once walked according to the course of this world, according to the prince of the power of the air, the spirit who now works in the sons of disobedience, among whom also we all once conducted ourselves in the lusts of our flesh, fulfilling the desires of the flesh and of the mind, and were by nature children of wrath, just as the others." To bring a spiritually dead person to faith in Christ is something that only God can do. It requires His omnipotent power. As Jesus Himself said, "No one can come to Me unless the Father who sent Me draws him" (John 6:44). We need the life-giving and heart-regenerating power of the sovereign Spirit to work true and saving faith in our rebellious hearts.

God calls sinners effectually through the preaching of the gospel. As the apostle said to the Thessalonians, "But we are bound to give thanks to God always for you, brethren beloved by the Lord, because God from the beginning chose you for salvation through sanctification by the Spirit and belief in the truth, *to which He called you by our gospel*, for the obtaining of the glory of our Lord Jesus Christ" (2 Thess. 2:13–14). The Canons of Dort summarize well how the Spirit uses the gospel to call us to Christ:

> But when God accomplishes his good pleasure in the elect, or works in them true conversion, he not only causes the gospel to be externally preached to them, and powerfully illumines their

> minds by his Holy Spirit, that they may rightly understand and discern the things of the Spirit of God; but by the efficacy of the same regenerating Spirit, pervades the inmost recesses of the man; he opens the closed, and softens the hardened heart, and circumcises that which was uncircumcised, infuses new qualities into the will, which though heretofore dead, he quickens; from being evil, disobedient and refractory, he renders it good, obedient, and pliable; actuates and strengthens it, that like a good tree, it may bring forth the fruits of good actions. (head 3/4, art. 11)

The Spirit's effectual calling of a sinner displays God's amazing grace, which Paul knew firsthand. Before he was called by God to faith in Christ, he was spiritually dead in his trespasses and sins. He was Saul of Tarsus, the violent persecutor of Christ's church. He deserved God's justice and wrath. Yet the Lord had mercy on him. Christ sought out Saul while he was traveling on the road to Damascus to arrest more Christians (Acts 9:1–9). He opened Saul's eyes to his guilt and showed him his need for a Savior. He regenerated his heart and gave him the gift of faith (Eph. 2:8–9). On top of that, he was "appointed a preacher, an apostle, and a teacher" of the gospel (2 Tim. 1:11). By reminding Timothy that he too had been effectually called by the Holy Spirit, he was helping him see that the gospel was worth suffering for.

The Gospel Includes Our Justification

Our salvation not only includes election and effectual calling but also our justification. Paul compresses this glorious doctrine, which he expounds so fully in his letters to the Romans and Galatians, in the simple statement that our salvation is "not according to our works" (1:9). He found it necessary to remind Pastor Titus of this same wondrous truth: "But when the kindness and the love of God our Savior toward man appeared, not by works of righteousness which we have done, but according to His mercy He saved us…that having been justified by His grace we should become heirs according to the hope of eternal life" (Titus 3:4–5a, 7). When we put our trust in Christ by the Spirit's grace, God imputes to us the perfect righteousness of His Son and declares that we are righteous and acceptable in His sight. Not even the remaining sin against which we must struggle all our lives can reverse this great act of God. He accepts us not because of *our* obedience but because of *Christ's* obedience. His good works are credited to us.

To illustrate this, imagine standing at the gates of heaven. You are met by an angel who checks to see if you are on the list of those worthy to enter. After asking your name, he finds it on the register and asks, "Are you *this* saint? It says here that you were always obedient to God. It says that you committed no sin. When you were reviled, you did not revile in return. When you suffered you did not threaten others but continued entrusting yourself to Him who judges justly. It says that you fed the hungry, welcomed strangers, clothed the naked, visited the sick, and went to those in prison. It says here that you loved the Lord your God with all your heart, soul, and mind and that you loved your neighbor as yourself. Is this you?"

You could then respond, "Yes, that is me by Christ's amazing grace," for God has given to you as a gift what Christ earned through His work.[5] It seems too good to be true, but that is the gospel.

As Paul stresses in 1:9 and elsewhere in his writings, our good works do not contribute to our salvation in any way. If they did, then we could never be assured of our salvation, for we would never know when we have done enough. This would be of no encouragement to Timothy at all. "But since Timothy's call is based on God's own purpose and grace," says William Mounce, "a grace that has obviously empowered Timothy, then Timothy can with full assurance meet the challenge of the Ephesian opponents."[6]

Knowing that God has justified us "not according to our works" but because of the works of Christ, we too can with full assurance meet the daily challenges of our opponents: the world, the flesh,

5. This sermon illustration was used by the late Rev. Andrew Cammenga, former pastor of the Escondido United Reformed Church.

6. Mounce, *Word Biblical Commentary*, vol. 46, 483.

and the devil. There is no greater contributing factor to our joy and comfort as Christians than the reality that God accepts us even though we still struggle with sin and failure. Knowing that God loves us on account of Christ protects us from the roller coaster of our own conscience and emotions. As Belgic Confession, article 23 puts it, "That is enough to cover all our sins and to make us confident, freeing the conscience from the fear, dread, and terror of God's approach, without doing what our first father, Adam, did, who trembled as he tried to cover himself with fig leaves."

The Gospel Includes our Sanctification

Paul says that God "called us with a holy calling" (1:9). Some English translations read "*to* a holy calling" instead of "*with* a holy calling" because the Greek word for "calling" can be translated with either preposition.[7] Both ways are true theologically: God calls us *with* a holy calling (i.e., the work of the Holy Spirit effectually calling a sinner to Christ) but also *to* a holy calling (i.e., a life of holiness). Paul seems to have the latter in view here. It harmonizes with Paul's exhortations in chapter 2: "Let everyone who names the name of Christ depart from iniquity" (v. 19), and "Flee also youthful lusts; but pursue righteousness, faith, love, and peace with those who call on the Lord out of a pure heart" (v. 22).

When God calls a person to Himself, He calls that person to be a disciple. He calls a sinner not only *from* a life of sin but also *to* a life of holiness. As Paul says in Romans 1:7 and 1 Corinthians 1:2, Christians are "called to be saints." To be a saint is to be holy. In 1 Thessalonians 4:7, he says that "God did not call us to uncleanness, but in holiness." God calls us to a holy life because He Himself is holy (1 Peter 1:15–16).

---

7. The adjective "holy" describes the cognate noun in the dative, "calling." As Towner notes, "The precise sense of the dative addition is not clear.... It may be a dative of means—'he called us *by means of* or *with* a holy calling,' the force of which would probably be to emphasize that it is a calling that comes *from* God.... Alternatively, the sense of the dative might be...to describe the goal of calling as 'to a holy life,' or to be 'those called saints.'" *Letters to Timothy and Titus*, 468.

This calling to holiness is part of the lifelong process of sanctification whereby the Holy Spirit is conforming us to the image of Christ. Like justification, sanctification is a gift from God earned for us by Christ. It is included in the benefits of salvation. The moment God justifies us through faith in Christ, He begins sanctifying us and producing in us good works to His glory. As the Belgic Confession states in its article 24 on the sanctification of sinners: "It is impossible for this holy faith to be unfruitful in a human being, seeing that we do not speak of an empty faith but of what Scripture calls 'faith working through love,' which leads a man to do of himself the works that God has commanded in his Word. These works, proceeding from the good root of faith, are good and acceptable to God, since they are all sanctified by his grace."

Knowing that the power of the Holy Spirit was at work in him, sanctifying him and producing good works to the glory of God, served as an encouragement to Timothy. And it serves as an encouragement to us as well.

The Gospel Includes Our Glorification

Finally, the apostle includes the doctrine of glorification in his statement in order to show Timothy why the gospel is worth suffering for. He draws Timothy's attention to another important aspect of our salvation by explaining that "our Savior Jesus Christ...has abolished death and brought life and immorality to light through the gospel" (1:10). As Walter Liefeld said, this part of the passage may be "perhaps the most powerful antidote to Timothy's timidity and tendency to shame."[8] What could be more encouraging to the Ephesian minister than to know that the Christ he serves has abolished death? The word that Paul uses for "abolished" (*katargeo*) is the same one used in 1 Corinthians 15:26: "The last enemy that will be destroyed is death." Christ abolished death through His

---

8. Walter Liefeld, *The NIV Application Commentary: 1 & 2 Timothy, Titus* (Grand Rapids: Zondervan, 1999), 239.

resurrection, securing for us glorified life and immortality in the new heavens and new earth.

Nowadays, death is not a welcome subject and is considered off limits. We simply don't bring it up in polite company. We don't even like using the word *death.* Instead of saying someone died, we use sugarcoated expressions like "he passed." We used to build cemeteries next to churches so that people on their way to worship were confronted with the sobering reality of death and the brevity of life. Now we put them on the outskirts of town, often in walled-off areas, so that we do not have to look at them. Open-casket funerals are also becoming a thing of the past. It was once the custom for a family to look on the body of their loved one as they paid their last respects. Today we are too squeamish for that. We don't want to think about death. It hits too close to home, reminding us too much of our own mortality. We prefer to live with the fiction that death isn't part of our world.

But in fact, death is a reality that no one can escape. It is the great foe of the human race, the curse for our sin and rebellion against our Creator (Genesis 3). Death is not a happy friend who helps us complete "the circle of life." It is a hostile enemy that disrupts our lives. It arrives with its massive, unforgiving jaws and swallows someone we love. No one is immune to this adversary. It is, as the prophet Isaiah said, "the covering cast over all people" and "the veil that is spread over all nations" (Isa. 25:7). Whether we are rich or poor, black or white, educated or uneducated is totally irrelevant: death comes for us all.

This is what makes Paul's words in 1:10 so comforting. Someone has come to rescue us from death—namely, "our Savior Jesus Christ, who has abolished death and brought life and immortality to light through the gospel." Christ earned eternal life through His perfect life, atoning death, and glorious resurrection. He opened up the way to the tree of life for all those who put their trust in Him. Although believers must still face death, they do so with the assurance that they will be raised from the dead on the last day and enter in to glorified life in the presence of the Lord. God has given them this promise (Isa. 25:6–9; John 11:25–26; Rom. 8:18–25; 1 Cor. 15:20–26, 50–55; 2 Cor. 5:1–5; Phil. 3:20–21; Col. 3:1–4; 1 Thess. 4:13–18). This means that for Christians, death has lost its sting and is no longer to be feared (Heb. 2:14–15).

It also means that life is not meant to be lived in some sort of hopeless hedonism, driven by a mad quest to find fulfillment through new experiences and pleasures. The wisdom of this world says, "Eat, drink, and be merry, for you only live once. Live it up while you can!" But the wisdom from above says, "Christ Jesus has been raised from the dead. He is the firstfruits of the whole resurrection harvest that will be manifest on the last day. The best is yet to come, 'so, whether you eat or drink, or whatever you do, do all to the glory of God'" (1 Cor. 10:31 ESV).

Until That Day

When Paul wrote these words to Timothy, he was in chains (2 Tim. 1:16; 2:9), lonely (4:9–11), awaiting trial after his preliminary hearing (1:16–17), and expecting to be executed (1:6–8). He was without the comfort of books or even a cloak to stay warm (1:13). And yet despite all his suffering, Paul remained full of hope. He was able to say from his prison cell, "Nevertheless I am not ashamed, for I know whom I have believed and am persuaded that He is able to keep what I have committed to Him until that Day" (1:12). For Paul, the gospel, that which had been entrusted to him as "a preacher, an apostle, and a teacher" (1:11), was too valuable to lose hope. The glorious benefits announced in its message—*election*, *effectual calling*, *justification*, *sanctification*, and *glorification*—make it worth suffering every discomfort and displeasure in this life. As he said to the church at Rome, "For I consider that the sufferings of this present time are not worthy to be compared with the glory which shall be revealed in us" (Rom. 8:18).

God has not promised us a comfortable life. We live in a fallen and broken world where suffering is a reality and Christianity is persecuted. If you are not suffering right now, you are near to someone who is, and someday you will suffer too. God has not promised that we will escape suffering, but He has promised Himself. He has promised to take all our guilt and plunge it into the black hole of Christ's atoning death. He has promised to finish in us the good work He began. He has promised to keep us from stumbling and to present us blameless before the presence of His glory with great joy (Jude 24). He has promised to award us with "the crown of righteousness…on that Day" (2 Tim. 4:8). He has not promised us a comfortable life, but He has promised us eternal life in the age to come. In light of such a great salvation, why wouldn't we, like our brothers and sisters did in the sixteenth century, offer our backs to stripes, our tongues to knives, our mouths to gags, and our whole bodies to the fire rather than deny the gospel?

May God strengthen us by His grace so that we too are unashamed of the testimony about our Lord and share in suffering for the gospel.

4

The Pattern of Sound Words

2 TIMOTHY 1:13–18

Hold fast the pattern of sound words which you have heard from me, in faith and love which are in Christ Jesus. That good thing which was committed to you, keep by the Holy Spirit who dwells in us.

This you know, that all those in Asia have turned away from me, among whom are Phygellus and Hermogenes. The Lord grant mercy to the household of Onesiphorus, for he often refreshed me, and was not ashamed of my chain; but when he arrived in Rome, he sought me out very zealously and found me. The Lord grant to him that he may find mercy from the Lord in that Day—and you know very well how many ways he ministered to me at Ephesus.

Italy is a nation passionate about its wine. Since the days of the Romans, wine has played a significant role in the country's culture. It is present at most meals and enjoyed daily by people from all classes of society. Beautiful vineyards can be found all over the Italian peninsula. The country boasts over 350 varieties of grapes, twenty wine-producing regions, and more than one million vineyards under cultivation, some of them among the world's oldest. Because Italians view wine as an important part of their daily life, they care deeply about perfecting the production process and protecting the quality of taste.

In order to safeguard the purity of their wine and preserve it for the next generation, Italy regulates its wine-making industry through a series of rigorous qualifications and government-issued quality assurance tags found on the necks of wine bottles. The highest classification among these labels is *DOCG*, which stands for *Denominazione di Origine Controllata e Garatita* (denomination of controlled and guaranteed origin). To obtain this label for a bottle of wine, Italian winemakers must meet strict standards pertaining to the location of the vineyard, production, quantity, alcohol content, aging, and taste. The variety of grape can be grown only within its original region, and the prescribed pattern of production must be followed precisely. This ensures that a good bottle of Barolo from Piedmont or Brunello di Montalcino from Tuscany is the genuine article and not a counterfeit. It also preserves the excellence of Italy's wines for future generations.

Italy's devotion to quality control of its wine illustrates Paul's concern to preserve the purity of the gospel message and ensure that it be brought to future generations. Convinced that the time of his death was near, the apostle writes with a great sense of urgency to Timothy, his young and trusted colleague. Paul had finished his race. Timothy must now carry the torch. In 2 Timothy 1:13–14, Paul exhorts Timothy to "hold fast the pattern of sound words which you have heard from me" and "that good thing which was committed to you, keep by the Holy Spirit who dwells in us." The Greek word he uses in verse 13 for "pattern" describes a model, form, or standard that serves as a trustworthy guide. After summarizing sound apostolic doctrine in 1:9–10, Paul tells Timothy to continue in this teaching and guard it. Like a disciplined Italian winemaker who refuses to deviate from the prescribed standard of production, Paul stresses to Timothy that he was not to dilute the gospel message or depart from the doctrine that was being entrusted to him. In one sense, the gospel that Timothy was to preach must bear the label *DOCG*. He was to follow the pattern of sound words and guard the good deposit.

Paul's plea for doctrinal purity is applicable in every age, including our own. The church must be vigilant to guard the gospel so that each generation can rediscover it. Although we live at a time when people do not "endure sound doctrine, but according to their own desires, because they have itching ears…heap up for themselves teachers" (4:3), we must follow the pattern of sound words, for it provides the church with nourishment, protects the church from heresy, and preserves the church's unity.

The Pattern of Sound Words Provides the Church with Nourishment

In 1:13, Paul commands Timothy, "Hold fast the pattern of sound words which you have heard from me." By "sound words," Paul means doctrine, teaching. He uses the same expression in his first letter to Timothy and equates it to good and orthodox doctrine: "If anyone teaches otherwise and does not consent to *wholesome words, even the words of our Lord Jesus Christ, and to the doctrine which accords with godliness*, he is proud, knowing nothing, but is obsessed with disputes and arguments over words, from which come envy, strife, reviling, evil suspicions, useless wranglings of men of corrupt minds and destitute of the truth, who suppose that godliness is a means of gain" (6:3–5). Sound, healthy doctrine nourishes the soul. As believers, we cannot grow in the grace and knowledge of Christ apart from sound doctrine.

Paul's concern in writing to Timothy was that the gospel and apostolic doctrine be preserved beyond the days of the apostles. The pattern of sound words would need to be followed by pastors like Timothy and the men whom he would train. The continuity between Paul's ministry and Timothy's is highlighted in the phrase "the things that you have heard from me" (2 Tim. 2:2; cf. 1:13). As Philip Towner put it, "It is precisely this apostolic continuity that ensures the purity of the message on into the next generation."[1]

One of the most important ways for the church to ensure the preservation of apostolic doctrine for future generations is through the use of time-tested creedal statements such as the Apostles' Creed. The word *creed* comes from the Latin *credo*, which simply means, "I believe." A creed is a summary of what one believes. The Apostles' Creed is an official and faithful summary of essential

1. Towner, *Letters to Timothy and Titus*, 477.

apostolic doctrine. It is named after the apostles not because the apostles themselves wrote it but because it codifies the apostolic message and helps us "connect the dots" of the Bible's teaching. It helps the church follow the pattern of sound words laid down by the apostles.

Additionally, the Protestant Reformation gave us confessions and rich catechisms so that the church would be nourished by sound doctrine. The Heidelberg Catechism, for example, published in 1563, exposits the Apostles' Creed line by line so that we are instructed in what we believe and why we believe it. It also teaches us what God requires of us in the Ten Commandments and what it means to pray the Lord's Prayer. It educates us about the law and the gospel and how we are to live in gratitude to God with a life of good works. It organizes biblical doctrine and teaches us in a question-and-answer format so that we will know the basics of Christianity. Likewise, the Westminster Shorter and Larger Catechisms are tools that help us follow the pattern of sound words. For centuries, the church has used these tools so that Christ's flock will be nourished in the faith and pass it on to the next generation.

We should not think of learning doctrine and confessing the faith as a dry, intellectual exercise. Paul tells Timothy that following the pattern of sound words is to be done "in faith and love which are in Christ Jesus" (1:13b). Philip Towner offers a helpful explanation of this latter part of verse 13: "'Faith and love' serve as an abbreviation for the authentic life of faith, combining into a unity the dimensions of one's relationship to God and the lifestyle of service produced by that faith-relationship. In short, for Timothy to 'keep' the apostolic message and proclaim it he must at the same time pay careful attention to his own faith in Christ."[2] Paul's counsel to Timothy in 1:13 is in perfect harmony with his exhortation to the Ephesian elders (a group of which Timothy was part) during his farewell discourse at Miletus: "Take heed to yourselves and to all the flock, among which the Holy Spirit has made you overseers,

2. Towner, *Letters to Timothy and Titus*, 478.

to shepherd the church of God which He purchased with His own blood" (Acts 20:28). Following the pattern of sound words requires of us more than a confession from our lips but also true faith in our hearts and, consequently, lives lived in love for God and neighbor.

The Pattern of Sound Words Protects the Church from Heresy

In 1:14, Paul exhorts Timothy, "That good thing which was committed to you, keep by the Holy Spirit who dwells in us." Not only is Timothy to follow the pattern of sound words so that the pure apostolic gospel will continue to be preached after Paul's death but he must also guard it against heresy (i.e., false teaching) and competing truth claims. This would require diligence from Timothy, for the church he served in Ephesus was under philosophical and theological attack, both externally and internally.

Externally, the gospel needed to be guarded against the claims of pagan religion and materialism. For example, Ephesus was home to the Temple of Artemis, one of the Seven Wonders of the Ancient World. The temple was not only the center of civic and religious life but it also made Ephesus a wealthy metropolis in the centuries leading up to the time of the apostles. Consequently, the city was, as Paul describes, filled with "lovers of themselves, lovers of money," and "lovers of pleasure rather than lovers of God" (3:2, 4).

Materialism and pagan religion, however, were not the only threats to the church in Ephesus. There was also a false teaching about Christianity circulating among some of the members. In Paul's first letter to Timothy, he issues an urgent warning about those who teach deviant doctrines contrary to the truth. It appears that this particular teaching included a misguided use of the Mosaic law (1:7) and speculative "fables and endless genealogies" (1:4) inspired by "deceiving spirits and doctrines of demons" (4:1). This doctrine was also legalistic in that it required of believers things that Scripture does not, such as forbidding marriage and demanding Christians "to abstain from foods which God created to be received with thanksgiving" (4:3). Those espousing this heresy, people such as Hymenaeus, Alexander (1:20), and Philetus (2 Tim. 2:17), had "made shipwreck of their faith"

(1 Tim. 1:19 ESV), "strayed concerning the truth" (2 Tim. 2:18), and were spreading irreverent babble "and contradictions of what is falsely called knowledge" (1 Tim. 6:20). By the time Paul wrote 2 Timothy, this heresy had developed further, including the claim that the resurrection had already happened (2 Tim. 2:17–18).

Following the pattern of sound words and guarding the good deposit against false teaching and competing truth claims have been a challenge for God's people in every age. In the Old Testament, Israel was threatened by the false religion of Egypt, a culture steeped in polytheism, the belief that there are many gods. The Egyptians had deities for every conceivable area of the universe. There was a god for fertility, for agriculture, for rain, for the sun, and so on. It was vital, therefore, for Israel to know and remember that there is only one true and living God, who alone is the creator and governor of the universe. Having spent four hundred years in Egypt, Israel needed protection against the false religion of polytheism. For this reason, God gave Israel a creed to recite and teach to their children: "Hear, O Israel: The LORD our God, the LORD is one!" (Deut. 6:4). Known as the Shema, this creed protected Israel against polytheism and helped guard the good deposit entrusted to them so that it would continue into future generations.

We also find creedal statements in the New Testament. For example, when Paul sought to protect the church at Corinth from the poisonous heresy that denied the bodily resurrection, he quoted a creed with which the Corinthians were familiar. He says, "For I delivered to you first of all that which I also received: that Christ died for our sins according to the Scriptures, and that He was buried, and that He rose again the third day according to the Scriptures" (1 Cor. 15:3–4). He then unpacks this brief creed throughout the rest of the chapter, explaining that one cannot deny the resurrection of the body without also denying the resurrection of Christ, which in turn is a denial of the gospel itself. Paul drew upon this well-known creed to protect Christ's flock from wolves and the heresy they taught.

At times the church has had to write new creeds in order to respond to new false teachings that arise within the church. For example, in the fourth century, the church faced a great crisis when a well-trained and popular preacher named Arius attacked the doctrine of the eternality and divinity of Christ. Believing that he was reading the Bible correctly and that he was acting in the interest of truth, he denied essential Christian doctrine and led many people astray. The church responded to this situation by examining Arius's teachings and rightly condemning them as heresy. Delegated church leaders from all over the Roman Empire gathered in the city of Nicaea and wrote a creed in response to Arian heresy in order to protect believers. That creed is known as the Nicene Creed and is still confessed by the church today.

As heresies arise and attack the truth in every age, it is necessary for the church to take Paul's plea to heart. We must follow the pattern of sound words and guard the good deposit. We must remember the words of the apostle John: "Beloved, do not believe every spirit, but test the spirits, whether they are from God; because many false prophets have gone out into the world" (1 John 4:1). By believing and confessing a clear system of biblical doctrine, the church is better equipped to warn and protect Christ's sheep.

Furthermore, creeds and confessions protect us from ourselves. As fallen people, each of us reads the Bible with philosophical presuppositions. We bring baggage to the text we are interpreting. While creeds and confessions do not guarantee that we will not interpret falsely a certain passage of Scripture, they nevertheless provide a safeguard. They are like the rails on which a train runs. Take away the rails, and you have a disaster. Likewise, when individual Christians try to read the Bible completely independently from the historic Christian church and refuse to check their interpretation with what the church has confessed through the ages, they are bound for disaster.

The Pattern of Sound Words Preserves the Church's Unity

It is sometimes said, "Doctrine divides, but love unites," or "Doctrine divides, but practice unites." The idea behind both of these statements is that an emphasis on doctrine will divide Christ's church by leading it into theological debates and disputes when instead the church should be focused on loving others and doing good works. Not long ago, one of the most popular evangelical leaders in America urged church leaders to pursue a new kind of reformation: "The first Reformation was about belief. This one needs to be about behavior.... We need a reformation not of creeds but deeds."[3]

To pit doctrine against love and practice, however, is to create a false dichotomy. Our unity as Christians is based on the truth we confess. Our responsibility to love one another and perform good works is always to be done *in response* to that truth. To divorce doctrine from love and good works is to profess a religion different from Christianity, for Christianity is based on the gospel of Jesus Christ. One cannot be a follower of Jesus without believing and confessing certain doctrines about Him: His incarnation, righteous life, atoning death, resurrection, and ascension. When Jesus commissioned His apostles to "make disciples of all the nations," He told them that doctrine ("teaching them to observe all things that I have commanded you") is an essential component of disciple making (see Matt. 28:16–20). Consequently, the first congregation that the apostles planted devoted themselves to the apostles' doctrine (Acts 2:42). The Christian church as a whole is built on the foundation of the apostles and prophets, Christ Jesus Himself being the cornerstone (Eph. 2:20). To neglect apostolic doctrine is to neglect the foundation of the church's unity. Rather, we are called to "keep the unity of the Spirit in the bond of peace," maintaining our fidelity to the truth that unites us: "There is one body and one Spirit, just as you were called in one hope of your calling; one Lord, one faith, one baptism; one God and Father of all, who is above all, and through all, and in you all" (Eph. 4:3–6).

Whenever we attempt to base our Christian unity on something other than the gospel, whether it is our political affiliations,

---

3. Trennis Henderson, "Rick Warren Challenges Baptists to Launch Reformation of Deeds, Not Creeds," *Religious Herald*, August 8, 2005, Baptist News Global, https://baptistnews.com/article/rickwarrenchallengesbaptiststolaunchreformationofdeedsnotcreeds/#.YPhEaehKiUm.

cultural practices, or consumer preferences, we are guilty of creating division in the body of Christ. This is precisely what some believers in Asia were doing in Paul's day. He writes in 2 Timothy 1:15, "This you know, that all those in Asia have turned away from me." By Asia Paul did not mean the continent of Asia as we know it today, but the Roman province in the first century that had as its capital the city of Ephesus and encompassed what is now western Turkey. It seems that several church leaders in the area had elevated their opinions about Paul over their fidelity to the truth, thus disrupting unity in the church: "among whom are Phygellus and Hermogenes," notes Paul (1:15). We know nothing about these two men other than what is mentioned here. They were part of the group that had defected from Paul, probably in embarrassment over his imprisonment and disavowal of his apostolic authority.

To follow the pattern of sound words requires a commitment to the body of Christ, regardless of our personal opinions about a particular member of the body. We cannot claim to love Jesus while at the same time despising His body. The church is not a club of like-minded individuals who stick together like a clique of teenage friends, but a real spiritual family created by God through the blood of Christ. Just as we did not pick our biological siblings, neither did we pick our brothers and sisters in the Lord. We love each other not because we are perfectly compatible or because we are irresistibly attracted to one another, but because of our union with Christ. We must accept that the church is messy in this life and put to death any utopian dreams of a perfect church. Phygellus and Hermogenes failed to do this. They exchanged their commitment to the body of Christ for their personal preferences and dreams of a better church—namely, one without the apostle Paul.

Dietrich Bonhoeffer warned Christians about the tendency of "visionary dreaming" in his 1938 classic on Christian community, *Life Together*. Writing while teaching at an underground seminary for the Confessing Church in Nazi Germany, Bonhoeffer said,

> He who loves his dream of a community more than the Christian community itself becomes a destroyer of the latter, even

> though his personal intentions may be ever so honest and earnest and sacrificial. God hates visionary dreaming; it makes the dreamer proud and pretentious. The man who fashions a visionary ideal of community demands that it be realized by God, by others, and by himself. He enters the community of Christians with his demands, sets up his own law, and judges the brethren and God Himself accordingly. He stands adamant, a living reproach to all others in the circle of brethren. He acts as if he is the creator of the Christian community, as if his dream binds men together. When things do not go his way, he calls the effort a failure. When his ideal picture is destroyed, he sees the community going to smash. So he becomes, first an accuser of his brethren, then an accuser of God, and finally the despairing accuser of himself.[4]

If you are fashioning a visionary ideal of Christian community and demanding that it be realized by God, repent and ask for His forgiveness. Do not go the route of Phygellus and Hermogenes. Remember that it is God, not our dreams and ideals, who has bound us together in fellowship and made us a family in Christ. We come to the church, therefore, not as demanders but as thankful recipients.

In 1:16–18, Paul expresses his gratitude for a man who did the opposite of Phygellus and Hermogenes: "The Lord grant mercy to the household of Onesiphorus, for he often refreshed me, and was not ashamed of my chain; but when he arrived in Rome, he sought me out very zealously and found me" (1:16–17). Onesiphorus understood what it meant to follow the pattern of sound words in the faith and love that are in Christ Jesus. He demonstrated his commitment to Christ's church by not abandoning Christ's apostle, even though the apostle was in chains and considered by society to be a criminal and enemy of Rome. He traveled far to find Paul and tend to his needs. "Such ought the faithful to be," said the early church father Chrysostom, "like Onesiphorus. Neither fear nor threats nor disgrace should deter them from assisting one another, standing by

4. Dietrich Bonhoeffer, *Life Together: The Classic Exploration of Faith in Community* (1938; repr., San Francisco: HarperOne, 2009), 27–28.

them and succoring them as in war."[5] May God strengthen us by His grace so that we too will be unashamed like Onesiphorus and remain committed to the body of Christ.

Paul prays that this man who found him in prison would also find mercy from the Lord: "The Lord grant to him that he may find mercy from the Lord in that Day—and you know very well how many ways he ministered to me at Ephesus" (1:18). These words have been the subject of some controversy over the years. That Paul tells Timothy to greet "the household of Onesiphorus" in 4:19 and not Onesiphorus himself has led some to draw the conclusion that Onesiphorus was dead at the time Paul wrote this letter. More controversial, however, is the claim by some commentators, particularly Roman Catholic writers, that 1:18 provides biblical evidence of prayers for the dead. This is an unjustified assumption. In the first place, Paul's referring to Onesiphorus in 1:16–18 and his household in 4:19 does not prove that the man was dead. It is entirely plausible that Paul wrote this way because Onesiphorus was still in Rome or in some other place away from his family in Ephesus. Paul's instruction to greet Onesiphorus's household may have been an expression of the apostle's appreciation for the family's sacrifice while Onesiphorus was away.[6] "More important," notes Patrick Fairbairn, "is the circumstance which the apostle adds respecting this good man, to show that what he did at Rome was no isolated thing, but a following out of the course he was wont to pursue at home: 'And how many things he ministered in Ephesus, thou knowest very well.'"[7]

---

5. Chrysostom, *Homilies on 2 Timothy*, 237.

6. George Knight observes that "Paul speaks in 1 Cor. 1:16 about a man's household while that person is still alive and in 2 Timothy about 'that day' in reference to those who are still alive, including himself alone (1:12) and with all believers (4:8). Furthermore, he can wish eschatological blessings for those who are still living (e.g., 1 Thess. 5:23b). Therefore, that Onesiphorus was alive and separated from his family is as possible as that he was dead." *Pastoral Epistles*, 386. See also Mounce, *Word Biblical Commentary*, vol. 46, 496–97.

7. Fairbairn, *Commentary on 1 & 2 Timothy and Titus*, 330.

God's Vineyard

Following the pattern of sound words and guarding the good deposit is the responsibility of the Christian church in every age. Just as Timothy had to carry the torch of the gospel into the next generation, so too must ministers, elders, and church leaders today. We need faithful men and women to guard the purity of the gospel and apostolic doctrine. And yet this success of the gospel does not rest with humans. Ultimately, it is God Himself who is the master winemaker. The vineyard belongs to Him, and He is committed to preserve it. Jesus Christ has promised to build His church and that not even the gates of hell shall prevail against it (Matt. 16:18). This should bring enormous encouragement to us, and especially to those set apart to preach the gospel. As John Stott reminds us, we need not be afraid:

> We may see the gospel opposed everywhere and apostolic doctrine ridiculed. We may have to watch an increasing apostasy in the church, as our generation abandons the faith of its fathers. Do not be afraid! God will never allow the light of the gospel to be finally extinguished. True, he has committed it to us, frail and feeble creatures. He has placed his treasure in brittle, earthenware vessels. And we must play our part in guarding and defending the truth. Nevertheless, in entrusting the deposit to our hands, he has not taken his own hands off of it. He himself is its final guardian, and *he* will preserve the truth which he has committed to the church. We know this because we know him in whom we have trusted and continue to trust.[8]

No matter what may happen to us in this world, we can follow the pattern of sound words with confidence in our God, who is the final guardian of the gospel and His church.

---

8. Stott, *Message of 2 Timothy*, 47.

5

Wanted: Soldiers, Athletes, and Farmers

2 TIMOTHY 2:1–7

You therefore, my son, be strong in the grace that is in Christ Jesus. And the things that you have heard from me among many witnesses, commit these to faithful men who will be able to teach others also. You therefore must endure hardship as a good soldier of Jesus Christ. No one engaged in warfare entangles himself with the affairs of this life, that he may please him who enlisted him as a soldier. And also if anyone competes in athletics, he is not crowned unless he competes according to the rules. The hardworking farmer must be first to partake of the crops. Consider what I say, and may the Lord give you understanding in all things.

In recent years, the expectations for what a pastor should be have changed dramatically. For centuries, ministers of the word were expected first and foremost to be scholars and expositors of the Bible. As John Owen wrote in the seventeenth century, "The first and principal duty of a pastor is to feed the flock by diligent preaching of the word."[1] Earlier that century, the Synod of Dort (1618–1619), in its adopted church order for the Reformed churches of the Netherlands, recognized the following as the biblically prescribed duties of a pastor: "The office of the ministers is to continue in prayer and the ministry of the Word, to administer the sacraments, to watch over their colleagues, the elders and deacons,

1. John Owen, *The True Nature of a Gospel Church and Its Government*, in *The Works of John Owen*, ed. William H. Goold (Edinburgh: Banner of Truth, 1991), 16:74.

together with the whole congregation, and finally to exercise church discipline with the elders and to see to it that everything is done decently and orderly."[2] The ministry of the word was understood as preaching, teaching, catechizing, pastoral visitation, and performing weddings and funerals. These were the duties that pastors were expected to fulfill faithfully, along with continuing in prayer and pursuing godliness.

Nowadays, however, it seems that it is not enough for a minister to be a faithful expositor of the Bible and undershepherd of Christ's flock. Today's pastor is expected to be a dynamic speaker, expert counselor, marriage therapist, visionary leader, church-growth expert, fundraiser, staff administrator, and team player with a warm and winsome personality that makes everyone at all times feel welcome, loved, and important. Consider the following qualifications published by churches in recent (and real) pastoral search advertisements:

- The pastoral candidate must be a confident leader with an intuitive understanding of individuals within the congregation.

- He must think strategically, must be culturally relevant, must be an effective visionary.

- Must be a decisive decision-maker and able to cast a vision with long-term vision and building expansion.

- We are looking for a man who believers are not able to resist because of the wisdom and spirit with which he speaks.

- Our next senior pastor must be a senior pastor in a large church, has grown a church, a demonstrated leader, has

---

2. Richard R. DeRidder, ed., *The Church Orders of the Sixteenth Century Reformed Churches of the Netherlands Together with Their Social, Political, and Ecclesiastical Context* (Grand Rapids: Calvin Theological Seminary, 1987), 548.

> a positive attitude, a team player, a consensus builder, he is genuine and authentic but doesn't wear his heart on his sleeve, culturally relevant, especially toward younger adult demographics, and has no outstanding unresolved issues. He is winsome, gracious, enthusiastic, discerning, confident but not arrogant, inspirational, creative, a communicator, a preacher, a teacher, a visionary, a delegator, develops a team, a trainer, he is technologically savvy, he promotes peace and unity without compromising doctrinal purity.

At the same time, many pastors suffer burnout by trying to live up to such unrealistic expectations. Ruled by their desires to please everyone and shaped by what the world and the modern church define as success, many pastors find the ministry to be an exhausting job full of disappointment and frustration.

This is what makes 2 Timothy 2:1–7 so timely for Christians today for both pastors and parishioners alike. Paul uses three different metaphors to describe what ministers are to be like. Rather than saying that a pastor should be a life coach, therapist, and visionary, Paul says that the man must be like a soldier, an athlete, and a farmer. Each of these images describes a different shade of faithfulness. This is important for us to consider as we think about what we should want in a pastor. Our desires should be the same as God's desires, and what God wants from the ministers of His word is faithfulness.

Strengthened by Grace

After noting the courage and faithfulness of Onesiphorus (2 Tim. 1:16–18), Paul resumes his charge to Timothy in 2:1: "You therefore, my son, be strong in the grace that is in Christ Jesus." He uses the present tense of the verb "be strong" to underscore the ongoing nature of its action. Timothy must continually draw his strength from the grace God has provided to him (and all believers) in Christ. God's grace is His undeserved favor freely bestowed on rebellious sinners who are in debt and rightly deserve God's wrath. This grace is "in Christ Jesus" because Christ earned the blessing for us through His life, death, and resurrection. It can be received in no other way but through faith in Him. Those who put their trust in Christ receive a new status and identity. They are "in Christ" as people whom God has justified, adopted, is sanctifying, and will one day glorify.

But how is one strengthened by God's grace? What exactly did Paul mean in his exhortation to Timothy in 2:1? This imperative connects to what the apostle previously said in 1:7: "For God has not given us a spirit of fear, but of power and of love and of a sound mind." Instead of offering Timothy clichés about courage and self-sufficiency, Paul reminded his younger colleague that God supplies believers with sufficient strength so that they can fulfill their callings. Paul used the passive voice in the verb "be strong" (i.e., "be strengthened") to emphasize that this grace is received. This strength comes not from ourselves but from "the grace that is in Christ Jesus" (2:1). To be strengthened by this grace, therefore, means to find our sufficiency in Christ by remembering our new identity and all that God has provided for us.

We are to remember that God's Spirit gives us power to persevere in this life, even in the midst of the most difficult trials and hardships. He provides us with love so that we can use our gifts not for the benefit of ourselves, but for others. He strengthens us with a sound mind/self-control so that we can learn to be self-disciplined in our thoughts and behavior, despite the discouragement of suffering or the threat of opponents. He makes His power available to us by the Holy Spirit not to make us look self-sufficient to the world, but to display His glory in weak and imperfect people. Whatever fears and challenges Timothy was facing in Ephesus, God's grace would be sufficient to see him through (cf. 2 Cor. 12:9). He could find in Christ Jesus the strength to be unashamed of the gospel and of Paul, the Lord's prisoner (2 Tim. 1:8). God's grace would strengthen him to follow the pattern of sound words and guard the good deposit entrusted to him (1:13–14).

Today, as much as in the first century, the church needs ministers who will look for strength not in themselves but in the grace that is in Christ Jesus. The church does not need celebrity pastors who ooze with self-confidence in their abilities. It needs humble servants of local congregations who, mindful of their own weakness, find their confidence in the word of God and their strength in Christ's grace. In fact, it is necessary that ministers feel weak in their callings, for it is then that God's power is made perfect. As Paul said to the Corinthians, "For when I am weak, then I am strong" (2 Cor. 12:10).

But it is not only pastors who need to be strengthened by the grace that is in Christ Jesus. This is a necessity for every believer. We need to be strengthened because our faith often wavers and feels weak. Faith feels differently during different seasons of life. Sometimes it feels strong and buoyant. Other times it feels weak and lifeless. But our feelings do not define our faith. The *object* of our faith does. And that object is Christ Jesus. "A little faith gives a whole Christ," said John Owen. He continued:

> He that hath the least faith hath as true an interest, though not so clear an interest, in the righteousness of Christ as the most steadfast believer. Others may be more holy than he, but not one in the world is more righteous than he; for he is righteous with the righteousness of Christ.... The lowest degree of true faith gives the highest completeness of righteousness. You, who have but a weak faith, have yet a strong Christ. So that, though all the world should set itself against your little faith, it should not prevail. Sin cannot do it; Satan cannot do it;—hell cannot do it. Though you take but weak and faint hold on Christ, he takes sure, strong, and unconquerable hold on you.... Jesus Christ takes special care of them that are weak in faith. On what account soever they are sick, and weak, and unable, this good Shepherd takes care of them. He shall rule, and they shall abide.[3]

Look to Christ and put your trust in Him! His strength will sustain you through every storm and trial of life.

---

3. John Owen, "The Strength of Faith," in *The Works of John Owen*, ed. William H. Gould (Edinburgh: Banner of Truth, 1968), 9:40.

Strengthened in Ability

In 2 Timothy 2:2 Paul tells Timothy, "And the things that you have heard from me among many witnesses, commit these to faithful men who will be able to teach others also." Not only was Timothy to guard the good deposit entrusted to him but he was also to entrust that same deposit to faithful ministers of the word so that the gospel would continue into the next generation. As John Stott observed, "Here, then, are the four stages in the handing on of the truth, which Paul envisages: from Christ to Paul, from Paul to Timothy, from Timothy to 'faithful men,' and from 'faithful men' to 'others also.' This is the true 'apostolic succession.' Certainly it would involve men, a line of 'faithful men' at that, but the succession from the apostles is to be more in the message itself than in the men who teach it."[4] Anticipating his death, Paul urges Timothy to carry the torch from the apostolic era into the postapostolic era and pass it on to other faithful men.

These faithful men must be "able to teach" (1 Tim. 3:2), possessing spiritual gifts for proclaiming the word of God and explaining it to others clearly. As Paul told Titus, a minister must hold firm to the trustworthy word "as he has been taught, that he may be able, by sound doctrine, both to exhort and convict those who contradict" (Titus 1:9). This means, first of all, that the pastor needs to study the Scriptures rigorously, regardless of the pressures and pace of daily life. A minister of the word must be an expert on the word and therefore give himself to constant study of the word. Apart from this, he will not be strengthened in his abilities and never truly "be able to teach others also."

Ministers must be gifted, trained, and constantly strengthened in their abilities to preach and teach apostolic doctrine. But they must also be faithful in their service. In 2:3–6, Paul turns to three metaphors to describe the kind of faithfulness for which Timothy and his fellow ministers were to strive.

---

4. Stott, *Message of 2 Timothy*, 51–52.

Strengthened for Loyalty

In 2:3 we find the first of the three metaphors that Paul employs to describe a faithful minister: "You therefore must endure hardship as a good soldier of Jesus Christ." Roman soldiers were a common sight in cities throughout the empire, not just in Rome where Paul was incarcerated, but also in Ephesus where Timothy served. It was a well-known fact that soldiers were required to be loyal to their overseeing officers and to the Senate and people of Rome. The Latin abbreviation *SPQR*, *Senatus Populusque Romanus*, was often tattooed on Roman soldiers as a symbol of their loyalty and to make it easier to identify any deserters who abandoned their post. Soldiers in the first century were required to be loyal.

The same is true of soldiers today. Those who serve in the United States military are required to take an oath of loyalty. Raising their right hand, they say publicly, "I do solemnly swear that I will support and defend the Constitution of the United States against all enemies, foreign and domestic; that I will bear true faith and allegiance to the same; and that I will obey the orders of the President of the United States and the orders of the officers appointed over me according to the regulations and Uniform Code of Military Justice. So help me God."[5] Soldiers are to be loyal in times of peace and times of war, in times of relative ease and times of suffering. They are to be, as the motto of the United States Marine Corps puts it, *semper fidelis*, "always faithful."

The analogy that Paul makes between soldiers and ministers concerns loyalty. In the same way soldiers are called to be loyal to their country and commanding officers, ministers of the word are called to be loyal to Christ and His gospel. Paul emphasized loyalty as an essential characteristic of the faithful minister because he knew that Timothy's loyalty would be tested as he took a stand against false teaching in the church. He was to "wage the good warfare" (1 Tim. 1:18). Paul also knew that one of the greatest dangers

5. "The US Military Oath of Enlistment," Military.com, https://www.military.com/join-armed-forces/swearing-in-for-military-service.html.

every pastor faces is the temptation to be more concerned about pleasing people than pleasing Christ. He warns Timothy in 2 Timothy 4:3–4, "For the time will come when they will not endure sound doctrine, but according to their own desires, because they have itching ears, they will heap up for themselves teachers; and they will turn their ears away from the truth, and be turned aside to fables." Ministers can be tempted to modify the apostolic message and tamper with the good deposit entrusted to them in order to suit the preferences of their hearers. In a culture that says bigger is better and the size of a congregation is the mark of success, pastors often feel great pressure to compromise their principles rather than suffer a loss in numbers.

A pastor's loyalty will be tested in many ways. If he preaches expository sermons through the Bible (i.e., *lectio continua*) rather than topical series, there will be occasions when he will have to preach on passages that he knows will not sit well with everyone in the pews. There will be instances when he will need to "convince, rebuke, [and] exhort" (2 Tim. 4:2) those who are in rebellion, risking damage to his reputation as a likeable guy. There will be times when he will need to stand up for what is right with regard to biblical doctrine or reverent worship, knowing that what is right and what is popular will not always be in sync. But a minister is not called to be popular. He is called to be faithful and loyal to Christ.

The motivation for such single-minded loyalty is to please Christ. Paul says in 2:4: "No one engaged in warfare entangles himself with the affairs of this life, that he may please him who enlisted him as a soldier." The implication was that Timothy was not to allow anything in his life to distract him from his focus on and loyalty to Christ, even if it meant foregoing some personal freedoms. This is one of the reasons why, in years past, it was common for a minister to live in a parsonage next to the church building rather than enjoy the comfort of a private home. A parsonage kept him near the congregation he served. It helped him stay focused on his calling. In the same way, ministers often wore clerical collars instead of civilian clothes. Resembling a fetter around the neck, the collar was a mark of the pastor's loyalty to Christ as a bondservant of the word.

There is a wider application of this verse to all believers. The call to loyalty is not limited to a pastor. Speaking of the calling that is common to all Christians, Paul says in 2 Corinthians 5:9: "Therefore we make it our aim, whether present or absent, to be well pleasing to Him." To some degree we are all soldiers of Jesus Christ. God calls all of us to take up the armor He provides (Eph. 6:10–20), for none of us can avoid spiritual warfare and the conflict against the world, the flesh, and the devil. God strengthens us with His grace so that we can persevere and endure suffering with loyalty to Christ.

Strengthened for Integrity

In 2 Timothy 2:5, Paul switches from the metaphor of a soldier to that of an athlete: "And also if anyone competes in athletics, he is not crowned unless he competes according to the rules." Every sport has rules. The rules of the game provide the boundaries of competition. And every sport has its champion, whether it is the MLB team that wins the World Series, the PGA golfer who wins the Master's Tournament, or the runner who finishes first in the Boston Marathon. In the Greco-Roman world, athletes competed for the prize of a wreath worn as a crown. They were also expected to compete according to the rules and follow strict regulations governing their training regimen. As athletes would compete in the Olympic or Isthmian Games, they would take oaths promising to compete with integrity. The moral standards of competition in the first century were very high.

Paul says that in the same way that athletes were expected to compete according to the rules, ministers of the gospel must have integrity, serving with a high moral standard. Like Paul, they must fight the good fight, finish the race, and keep the faith (2 Tim. 4:7). They must "press toward the goal for the prize of the upward call of God in Christ Jesus" (Phil. 3:14). A minister must always strive to exemplify the qualities of an overseer listed in 1 Timothy

3:2–5—namely, that he “be blameless, the husband of one wife, temperate, sober-minded, of good behavior, hospitable, able to teach; not given to wine, not violent, not greedy for money, but gentle, not quarrelsome, not covetous.” Far more important than a pastor’s popularity or perceived success as a church grower, conference speaker, or published author is his integrity to labor like a self-disciplined athlete in the fear of the Lord.

We should add that to serve with integrity means that ministers need to do their own work. Because of the accessibility the internet provides, plagiarizing sermons has become easier than ever. It is not uncommon for pastors to use prepackaged sermon series available online. Christians complain of hearing the identical sermon (text, outline, illustrations, and all) from more than one preacher, without any acknowledgment that the work was not original. Such behavior is shameful and unbecoming of a minister, who is called to labor with integrity. His calling is to study the Scriptures as “a worker who does not need to be ashamed, rightly dividing the word of truth” (2 Tim. 2:15). Stealing another man’s work, however, is shameful. It is no less scandalous than the professional athlete who uses performance-enhancing drugs or bets against his own team. God wants His church led by men with integrity and self-discipline, not phonies who are merely putting on a show and keeping up appearances.

Like the metaphor of a good soldier in 2:3–4, the image of a disciplined athlete in verse 5 has a broader application for all Christians. The Bible calls every child of God to persevere in the faith like a self-disciplined athlete who competes with integrity. Hebrews 12:1–2 tells us, “Therefore we also, since we are surrounded by so great a cloud of witnesses, let us lay aside every weight, and the sin which so easily ensnares us, and let us run with endurance the race that is set before us, looking unto Jesus, the author and finisher of our faith.” In 1 Corinthians 9:24–25, Paul says, “Do you not know that those who run in a race all run, but one receives the prize? Run in such a way that you may obtain it. And everyone who competes for the prize is temperate in all things. Now they do it to obtain a perishable crown, but we for an imperishable crown." God strengthens us with His grace so that we can persevere and endure suffering with integrity.

Strengthened for Constancy

In 2 Timothy 2:6, Paul uses a third metaphor to describe the minister's faithfulness: "The hardworking farmer must be first to partake of the crops." A soldier must serve with loyalty, an athlete must play with integrity, and the farmer must work with constancy. Good farming depends as much on a farmer's relentless work ethic as it does on good soil and weather. This was especially true in the ancient world before the rise of mechanized equipment.

Paul says that the hardworking farmer is a model for ministers to emulate. An outstanding work ethic is necessary for the ministry. The pastor must stay focused on the tasks to which he has been called: continuing in prayer, laboring in the word (Acts 6:4; 1 Tim. 5:17; 2 Tim. 4:1–5), administering the sacraments, catechizing the youth, and assisting the elders in shepherding and disciplining the congregation. He must also preach the gospel like a farmer sowing seeds for a future crop, for he has been sent out as a laborer into the Lord's harvest (Matt. 9:37–38; cf. John 4:35; Rom. 1:13). God uses the means of His word to bring a harvest of souls. As Paul told the Corinthians, "I planted, Apollos watered, but God gave the increase. So then neither he who plants is anything, nor he who waters, but God who gives the increase" (1 Cor. 3:6–7). Ministers of the gospel can be confident that the Lord will use their labors and graciously reward them, which seems to be the allusion in the apostle's words in 2:6 that the farmer "must be first to partake of the crops."

Like the metaphors of soldier and athlete, the analogy of the hardworking farmer in 2:6 has an application for the whole church. Every believer is called to sow to the Spirit rather than the flesh (Gal. 6:8). We are promised that "the fruit of righteousness is sown in peace by those who make peace" (James 3:18). As the Anglican bishop J. C. Ryle said, Christians must cultivate the field of godliness through their diligent use of the means of grace and discipleship:

> I will never shrink from declaring my belief that there are no "spiritual gains without pains." I should as soon expect a farmer to prosper in business who contented himself with sowing his fields and never looking at them till harvest, as expect a believer to attain much holiness who was not diligent about his Bible-reading, his prayers, and the use of his Sundays. Our God is a God who works by means, and He will never bless the soul of that man who pretends to be so high and spiritual that he can get on without them.[6]

There is a sense in which every disciple of Christ is to work like a farmer, working with constancy in the cultivation of holiness.

Think Over What I Say

The analogies of soldier, athlete, and farmer warrant our reflection. Paul adds an imperative in 2:7: "Consider what I say, and may the Lord give you understanding in all things." Timothy was to consider carefully these three models of service and suffering for the gospel. So too must the church today. Pastors need to remember their calling as ministers of the word. They are not called to reach for the stars, be celebrities, or meet unrealistic expectations. They are called by God to be faithful in the duties of feeding Christ's flock and tending His sheep. Ministers of the gospel should return frequently to these three models of service in 2:3–6 and meditate on them. They would also do well to remember their vows and the charge given to them on the day of their ordination. The Form for Ordination of Ministers of the Word and Sacraments used by the United Reformed Churches in North America issues the following charge:

> Beloved brother and fellow servant in Christ, take heed to yourself and to all the flock, in which the Holy Spirit has made you a guardian, to feed the church of the Lord which he obtained with his own blood. Love Christ and feed his sheep,

---

6. J. C. Ryle, *Holiness: Its Nature, Hindrances, Difficulties, and Roots* (London: James Clarke, 1952), 21.

> exercising oversight, not under compulsion, but willingly, not for shameful gain, but eagerly, and not domineering over those in your charge, but humbly serving all. Set the believers an example in speech and conduct, in love, in faith, in purity. Attend to the public reading of Scripture, to preaching, and to teaching. Do not neglect the gift you have. Take heed to your teaching. Be patient in all trials. Be a good soldier of Jesus Christ, for by so doing you will save both yourself and your hearers. And when the Chief Shepherd appears, you will obtain the unfading crown of glory.[7]

Of course, no man is sufficient for these things, which is precisely why every minister must "be strong in the grace that is in Christ Jesus" (2:1). Men enter the ministry inadequately aware of how dependent they are on the Lord's grace. They will never outgrow their dependency on His grace even ten, twenty, and thirty years after the day of their ordination. It is incumbent upon pastors that they anchor their hope in Christ. The only way they can be faithful to the Lord is by being strengthened by the grace that is in Christ Jesus.

Likewise, congregants must heed the words of the apostle in 2:7: "Consider what I say, and may the Lord give you understanding in all things." What do you expect from your pastor? What do you want him to be? Are you frustrated with him because he is not meeting all of your personal expectations or satisfying your list of felt needs? His calling is not to be your best friend, life coach, or marriage therapist. His calling is to be faithful in feeding you with the word of God. Far more important than his ability to think strategically, be an effective visionary, or even be a dynamic speaker is his loyalty to Christ like a good soldier, his integrity like a self-disciplined athlete, and his constancy like a hardworking farmer. This is what we should expect of him. We should think over what Paul says in these words.

---

7. *Liturgical Forms and Prayers of the URCNA* (Wellandport, Ontario: URCNA, 2018), 71–72.

It would also serve congregations well to reflect from time to time on the charge that was given to them at the time of their pastor's ordination or installation (assuming that such a wise and time-tested practice was performed). The Form for Ordination of Ministers of the Word and Sacraments used by the United Reformed Churches in North America gives the following charge to the congregation immediately after the charge to the new minister:

> And you, beloved Christians, receive your minister in the Lord with all joy, and hold him in honor. Remember that through him God Himself speaks to you. Receive the Word that he, according to the Scripture, shall preach to you, not as the word of men, but, as it is in truth, the Word of God. Let the feet of those who preach the gospel of peace, and bring the good news, be beautiful and pleasant to you. "Obey your leaders and submit to them, for they are keeping watch over your souls, as those who will have to give an account. Let them do this with joy and not with groaning, for that would be of no advantage to you" (Heb. 13:17). If you do these things, the God of peace shall enter your homes. You who receive this man in the name of a prophet, shall receive a prophet's reward, and through faith in Jesus Christ, the inheritance of eternal life.[8]

Take heed to these words, Christian. Pray for your pastor. Do not pray that he will meet all of your expectations but that he will be faithful in his duties to preach the gospel and bring Christ to you in word and sacrament week after week. Pray that he will be faithful like a soldier, an athlete, and a farmer. If your pastor is faithful in these things, thank God for him. Do not be critical of him because of the gifts he does not possess; rather, be thankful for those which he does. Above all, pray that he will continue to be strengthened by the grace that is in Christ Jesus.

Remember too that your pastor is not the one to whom the church is married—Christ is. The pastor's job is simply to bring us to Christ and remind us of our identity in Him. Christ is the one

---

8. *Liturgical Forms and Prayers of the URCNA*, 72.

we need. Ultimately, He is the one who was loyal like a good soldier, fulfilling perfectly the Father's will. He lived with flawless integrity like a self-disciplined athlete, meriting the righteousness we need to stand blamelessly before God. He worked with constancy like a devoted farmer, accomplishing all the work the Father gave Him to do. He, and not our pastor, is the Shepherd who laid down His life for His sheep. Put your trust in Him, and thank Him for those ordinary, fallen, and flawed men He has called to feed your soul and labor like soldiers, athletes, and farmers.

6

Your Best Life Later

2 TIMOTHY 2:8–13

Remember that Jesus Christ, of the seed of David, was raised from the dead according to my gospel, for which I suffer trouble as an evildoer, even to the point of chains; but the word of God is not chained. Therefore I endure all things for the sake of the elect, that they also may obtain the salvation which is in Christ Jesus with eternal glory.

This is a faithful saying:

For if we died with Him,
We shall also live with Him.
If we endure,
We shall also reign with Him.
If we deny Him,
He also will deny us.
If we are faithless,
He remains faithful;
He cannot deny Himself.

In his runaway best seller *Your Best Life Now: Seven Steps to Living at Your Full Potential*, author Joel Osteen claims that God wants to help us become more successful in life. According to Osteen, one of the keys to success is found in our obedience to God: "If you will simply obey His commands, He will change things in your favor."[1] Another key is that we have to believe that God will give us favor

1. Joel Osteen, *Your Best Life Now: Seven Steps to Living at Your Full Potential* (New York: Warner Books, 2004), 119.

in every circumstance. "Perhaps you're searching for a parking spot in a crowded lot," Osteen illustrates. "Say, 'Father, I thank you for leading me and guiding me. Your favor will cause me to get a good spot.'"[2] We should also expect other people to do good things for us. "I've come to expect to be treated differently," says Osteen. "I've learned to expect people to want to help me. My attitude is: I'm a child of the Most High God. My Father created the whole universe. He has crowned me with favor, therefore, I can expect preferential treatment."[3] Additionally, we need to develop a healthy self-image. "God didn't make you to be average. God created you to excel." Therefore, "if you will start acting like it, talking like it, seeing yourself as more than a conqueror, you will live a prosperous and victorious life."[4]

Osteen's message of self-help and positive thinking is completely foreign to anything we find in Paul's letters. In fact, it is hard to imagine the weathered apostle recognizing any of Osteen's keys to successful Christian living. Here, in his last letter to Timothy, Paul does not tell his beloved son in the faith that he should "expect preferential treatment" in daily life or that God will change his circumstances to his favor. Instead, Paul has said a lot about suffering for Christ. So far in 2 Timothy, he has exhorted his colleague to share in "the sufferings for the gospel according to the power of God" (1:8) and to "endure hardship as a good soldier of Jesus Christ" (2:3). Paul has explained that it is because of the gospel that he was suffering as a criminal (1:10–12).

He still has more to say about suffering for Christ (3:12; 4:5), but here in 2:8–13, the aged missionary makes another appeal to endure hardship for the sake of the gospel. To strengthen his exhortation to Timothy, Paul uses three examples: first, the Lord Jesus (2:8); then, himself as an apostle (2:9–10); and finally, that all believers must persevere in the faith and endure to the end (2:11–13). In one sense, Paul tells Timothy, "You cannot have your best life now. Your

2. Osteen, *Your Best Life Now*, 41.
3. Osteen, *Your Best Life Now*, 39.
4. Osteen, *Your Best Life Now*, 82–83.

best life does not come this side of glory." Glory doesn't come when we land the job we really want, buy the perfect home, or get all the right pieces in place. Those are wonderful blessings from our benevolent Father in heaven, but they do not equal glory. Glory comes in the resurrection. "Be encouraged," says Paul, "your best life will come later, with eternal glory. Until then, press on! Endure to the end!"

In order to do that with courage, we must heed Paul's words in these verses and consider the person and work of Christ, be confident in the power of the word, and be comforted by the promise of glory.

Consider the Person and Work of Christ

In 2 Timothy 2:8 Paul says, "Remember that Jesus Christ," the One who suffered and died, "was raised from the dead." Paul uses a Greek participle that emphasizes the fact that Jesus is still risen. In other words, Christ's decisive and irreversible triumph over death will encourage Timothy as he walks the pathway of suffering for the gospel. We must remember the pattern of Christ's life: it was suffering first, glory later. First the cross, then the resurrection. First a crown of thorns, then a crown of glory. As those united with Christ, believers are being conformed to His image (Rom. 8:17; Phil. 3:10; 1 Peter 4:13). The pattern for our lives this side of glory, therefore, is cruciform, cross-shaped.

Paul's additional description of Jesus as "the seed of David" is a major theme in the New Testament (Matt. 1:1; 2:5–6; 22:41–45; Mark 12:35–37; Luke 20:41–44; Acts 2:25–36; 13:23; Rev. 22:16). It is based on God's covenant promises to David that his descendant would build the house of the Lord and be given an eternal kingdom (2 Samuel 7; cf. 23:5; 2 Kings 8:19; 2 Chron. 13:5; 21:7; Pss. 89:3; 132:11; Isa. 55:3; Jer. 33:20–21).

In the opening scenes of the New Testament, we discover Israel eagerly waiting for their promised king. There had not been a ruler on the Davidic throne for over five hundred years, since Nebuchadnezzar destroyed the temple in 586 BC. They longed for the day when the Lord would send the Messiah, the anointed son of David, to save them from their enemies and restore the kingdom. It was into this atmosphere of anticipation that the angel Gabriel's words of hope were declared to the young virgin Mary about her unborn son: "He will be great, and will be called the Son of the Highest; and the Lord God will give Him the throne of His father David. And He will reign over the house of Jacob forever, and of His kingdom there will be no end" (Luke 1:32–33). Jesus came into this world as the offspring of David, the builder of the house of God and the rightful heir to the eternal throne.

Christ entered into glory, however, through suffering. As the Davidic Messiah,

> He is despised and rejected by men,
> A Man of sorrows and acquainted with grief.
> And we hid, as it were, our faces from Him;
> He was despised, and we did not esteem Him. (Isa. 53:3)

As Jesus Himself told His disciples on the road to Emmaus, "Ought not the Christ to have suffered these things and to enter into His glory?" (Luke 24:26). Although Jesus alone suffered the wrath of God and atoned for our sin, we have nevertheless been called to suffer for Christ and follow His example as those united with Him in His death and resurrection (Phil. 3:10; 1 Peter 2:21; 3:13–19).

Our conformity to the image of Christ does not mean that life is little more than a depressing trudge through a dark valley where we encounter one horrific scene of suffering after another. Although it is true that this fallen world can resemble a valley of tears, not everything in the valley is sad. God has furnished the valley with beauty and joy. He supplies us with good gifts. We simply must keep in mind that, as Christians, we are not promised our best life right now. We will suffer in this life, and we should not be surprised when we do, whether it is sickness, loss, poverty, loneliness, disappointment, or persecution. "Yet in all these things we are more than conquerors through Him who loved us" (Rom. 8:37). Christ's resurrection is the dawn of the new creation in which believers now participate. So remember Jesus Christ as the offspring of David and the fulfillment of the Old Testament. Remember that He is the one who has been raised from the dead and ascended into heaven, where He is praying for you and interceding for you even as you endure hardship. Remember Him as you come to the Table and hear His words, "Do this in remembrance of Me." Consider the person and work of Christ and keep your eyes fixed on Him.

The person and work of Jesus Christ, the offspring of David who was raised from the dead, is the very substance of Paul's gospel. In 2:8 he calls it "my gospel" (as he does in Romans 2:16 and 16:25) not because he is its author, but because Christ appointed him to be an apostle and official steward of this glorious message.

Be Confident in the Power of the Word

In 2 Timothy 2:9–10, Paul cites a second example of suffering: himself. Being an apostle did not make him immune to sorrow. In fact, it was precisely because of the gospel that he was incarcerated and bound like a criminal. We have no reason to think that Paul enjoyed suffering. When he had the opportunity to avoid unlawful beatings by invoking his Roman citizenship, he did so (Acts 22:25–29; cf. 16:37). Nevertheless, Paul recognized that the principle of *suffering first, glory later* was a necessary part of his experience as an apostle and Christian. He explains, "Therefore I endure all things for the sake of the elect, that they also may obtain the salvation which is in Christ Jesus with eternal glory" (2:10).

Paul's suffering made him the target of criticism. To most onlookers, his life did not seem to be blessed by God. In the first-century Greco-Roman world, people's gods were supposed to protect them from misfortune. But when most people looked at Paul, they did not perceive a person who was receiving protection and provision from his God. For nearly three decades, Paul's apostolic ministry was punctuated with imprisonments, whippings, and danger. He was accustomed to hunger, dehydration, extreme cold, and severe heat (2 Cor. 11:23–27). None of his three missionary journeys went as planned. From a human perspective, there were major setbacks. He was reviled in Antioch (Acts 13:45), left for dead in Lystra (14:19), severely beaten in Philippi (16:23); chased out of Thessalonica (17:5–9); mocked in Athens (17:32); opposed in Corinth (18:6); accused of turning people away from false gods, resulting in a riot in Ephesus (19:23–29); dragged through the streets in Jerusalem (21:27–36); shipwrecked on Malta (27:13–44); and jailed for years in Rome. Nowadays people would say, "That guy must have a lot of bad karma!" Even many professing Christians in Paul's day seemed ashamed of his affliction and apparent weakness. If he was a true apostle of Jesus Christ, why did he suffer so much? To the human eye, his life seemed more cursed than blessed.

Contrary to the claims of his opponents, though, Paul's sufferings were not proof that God was against him but rather evidence that God was fulfilling His promise to sanctify him and conform him to the image of Christ. The Lord Jesus had said of Paul many years earlier, "He is a chosen vessel of Mine to bear My name before Gentiles, kings, and the children of Israel. For I will show him how many things he must suffer for My name's sake" (Acts 9:15–16). Every affliction Paul experienced was God's investment to bear fruit to His glory. Every form of weakness was an opportunity for God's grace to be at work in him. He took comfort in the Lord's promise, "My grace is sufficient for you, for My strength is made perfect in weakness." Paul, therefore, could say with confidence, "Most gladly I will rather boast in my infirmities, …in reproaches, in needs, in persecutions, in distresses, for Christ's sake. For when I am weak, then I am strong" (2 Cor. 12:9–10).

In his weakness, Paul could see more clearly the power of God's word at work: "I suffer trouble as an evildoer, even to the point of chains; but the word of God is not chained" (2 Tim. 2:9). His imprisonment could not deter the progress of the gospel. Despite all of Satan's efforts to hinder the gospel by afflicting its servants, the word is always at work in the world. It cannot be stopped. The first time Paul was imprisoned in Rome, he wrote to the church of Philippi and explained, "But I want you to know, brethren, that the things which happened to me have actually turned out for the furtherance of the gospel, so that it has become evident to the whole palace guard, and to all the rest, that my chains are in Christ; and most of the brethren in the Lord, having become confident by my chains, are much more bold to speak the word without fear" (Phil. 1:12–14). Even if its preachers and apostles are incarcerated, the word is always unbound, unchained, and free.

We too, therefore, can say with the apostle, "I am not ashamed of the gospel of Christ, for it is the power of God to salvation for everyone who believes" (Rom. 1:16). We can sing with confidence and conviction the words penned by Martin Luther in his famous hymn "A Mighty Fortress Is Our God":

> And though this world, with devils filled,
> Should threaten to undo us,
> We will not fear, for God has willed
> His truth to triumph through us.
> The prince of darkness grim,
> We tremble not for him;
> His rage we can endure,
> For lo! his doom is sure;
> One little word shall fell him.

Be Comforted by the Promise of Glory

In 2 Timothy 2:11–13, Paul cites one of the five faithful sayings that appear in the Pastoral Epistles (see 1 Tim. 1:15; 3:1; 4:8–9; Titus 3:8). This one was probably a contemporary Christian hymn, perhaps used in baptismal liturgies:

> For if we died with Him,
> We shall also live with Him;
> If we endure,
> We shall also reign with Him;
> If we deny Him,
> He also will deny us.
> If we are faithless,
> He remains faithful;
> He cannot deny Himself.

Notice how the saying moves from comfort to challenge and back to comfort. First, there is the promise of glory because of our union with Christ: "For if we died with Him, we shall also live with Him" (v. 11). When Jesus died on the cross, we died with Him in the sense that He was our representative, having our sins imputed to Him. Our guilt and condemnation were put to death through His death. When He was raised from the dead on the third day, we were raised with Him and seated in the heavenly places in the same representative manner (Rom. 6:1–11; Gal. 2:20; Eph. 2:1–10). Believers already live in the present as members of the world that is yet to be. "Therefore, if anyone is in Christ, he is a new creation; old things have passed away; behold, all things have become new" (2 Cor. 5:17). This new-age reality was inaugurated by the resurrection of Jesus.

Yet we still await the completion of our salvation, the resurrection of our bodies (Rom. 8:18–25; 1 Cor. 15:12–57; Phil. 3:20–21). This is the hope of glory all believers enjoy, a living hope that holds the future in the present because it is anchored in the past (1 Peter 1:3). Only this kind of hope can truly withstand the tempestuous onslaughts of persecution and sorrow in this present evil age.

Having been raised to newness of life, we are called to endure for Christ. Verse 12 challenges us to persevere to the end: "If we endure, we shall also reign with Him." George Knight beautifully summarizes the New Testament's teaching concerning this endurance: "Believers endure hatred by all for Christ's sake (Matt. 10:22 par. Mark. 13:13; cf. Matt. 24:13), they persevere in tribulation (Rom. 12:12), they endure great sufferings (Heb. 10:32) and temptation (Jas. 1:12), and they patiently endure suffering for doing good (1 Pet. 2:20). This endurance is to continue throughout their lives, as the use of the present tense shows."[5] The promise for those who endure to the end and do not apostatize is that they will reign with Christ in glory. "The Christian life is depicted as a life of dying, a life of enduring," says John Stott. "Only if we share Christ's death on earth, shall we share his life in heaven. Only if we share his

5. Knight, *Pastoral Epistles*, 404.

sufferings and endure, shall we share his reign in the hereafter. For the road to life is death, and the road to glory suffering."[6]

Verse 13 shifts back to comfort: "If we are faithless, He remains faithful." How this promise must have comforted Timothy, who was prone to timidity and needed encouragement. Feeling the great weight of responsibility to serve the churches amid suffering and persecution, Timothy would have found it easy to be filled with trepidation. "What if I am unfaithful? What if I fail? What if I turn back like so many others?" Paul, therefore, redirects Timothy's eyes to Jesus and *His* faithfulness. Left to ourselves, we would fall from the grace of God. But our Good Shepherd has promised, "My sheep hear My voice, and I know them, and they follow Me. And I give them eternal life, and they shall never perish; neither shall anyone snatch them out of My hand. My Father, who has given them to Me, is greater than all; and no one is able to snatch them out of My Father's hand" (John 10:27–29). Our strength is not found in ourselves, but in Christ. Our confidence is not in our own faithfulness, but in God's faithfulness to His promises.

There are some things that God *cannot* do. He cannot lie. He cannot change. He cannot sin. He cannot go against His promises. And, as Paul tells Timothy in 2:13, "He cannot deny Himself." What does it mean, though, that God cannot deny Himself? As the church father Augustine put it, "The only thing the Almighty cannot do is what He does not will.... Justice, after all, cannot have the will to do what is unjust, or wisdom will what is foolish, or truth will what is false."[7] In other words, God can *only* be faithful. He cannot be unfaithful. Satan knows this, which is why he did everything he could to get Adam to disobey God. Satan knew that because God said, "for in the day that you eat of [the tree of the knowledge of good and evil] you shall surely die" (Gen. 2:17) He would keep His promise, for God always keeps His promises.

---

6. Stott, *Message of 2 Timothy*, 63–64.

7. Augustine, "Sermons 214.4," in *Ancient Christian Commentary on Scripture*, 246.

This should fill us with confidence and courage as we face every trial and temptation. God has promised "that if you confess with your mouth the Lord Jesus and believe in your heart that God has raised Him from the dead, you will be saved" (Rom. 10:9). Rather than rely on the power of positive thinking to find our best life now, we can rest in God's promise that in every trial we face His grace is sufficient (2 Cor. 12:9).

> When through the deep waters I call you to go,
> The rivers of sorrow shall not overflow;
> For I will be with you, your troubles to bless,
> And sanctify to you your deepest distress.
>
> When through fiery trials your pathway shall lie,
> My grace, all sufficient, shall be your supply;
> The flame shall not hurt you; I only design
> Your dross to consume and your gold to refine.

7

A Workman for the Gospel

2 TIMOTHY 2:14–19

Remind them of these things, charging them before the Lord not to strive about words to no profit, to the ruin of the hearers. Be diligent to present yourself approved to God, a worker who does not need to be ashamed, rightly dividing the word of truth. But shun profane and idle babblings, for they will increase to more ungodliness. And their message will spread like cancer. Hymenaeus and Philetus are of this sort, who have strayed concerning the truth, saying that the resurrection is already past; and they overthrow the faith of some. Nevertheless the solid foundation of God stands, having this seal: "The Lord knows those who are His," and, "Let everyone who names the name of Christ depart from iniquity."

Within the walls of the Sforza Castle in Milan, Italy, stands an unfinished marble sculpture that attracts the attention of art lovers from around the world. Although at first glance its appearance may seem rudimentary and unimpressive, its craftsmanship becomes deeply respected when the viewer knows the identity of the sculptor. Known as the *Rondanini Pietà*, the statue is the product of the great Michelangelo Bounarroti, one of the giants of the Italian Renaissance. Michelangelo worked on the piece from 1552 until his death in 1564, never bringing it to completion. To study the figure in light of Michelangelo's more famous works increases one's appreciation for the labor and design it reveals. The same hands that sculpted the *Bacchus*, the *Madonna and Child*, and the iconic *David*, which stands in Florence's Galleria dell'Accademia as an internationally recognized masterpiece, also worked intensely on this column of Carrara marble. It is not difficult to imagine Michelangelo covered in sweat and white dust, striking his chisel into the stone with his hammer, using the routine count of seven blows followed by a four-count of rest, searching for lines that would become perfectly formed arms, legs, torso, and head. There is no shame in the unfinished product of *Rondanini Pietà*, for Michelangelo was a competent workman known for rightly handling marble.

In similar fashion, the faithful minister of the word is called to be a competent workman for the gospel, rightly handling the word of truth. This is the imagery Paul uses in his exhortation to Timothy in 2:14–19. Thus far in his letter, Paul had used three metaphors to describe a faithful pastor: he must be a self-sacrificing soldier, a self-disciplined athlete, and a self-denying farmer. He now adds a fourth: he must be an approved, unashamed, and competent workman. He is not called to be famous like Michelangelo nor produce sermons that will be recognized by others as masterpieces. But, like Michelangelo, he should labor in his craft with skill, devotion, and diligence, for it is through the minister's work that Christ is building up His church in the world.

Understanding Paul's words in this passage is important for pastors and parishioners alike, for it helps everyone in Christ's church to have proper and biblical expectations of the minister and his work. Ministers of the word should be liberated from false expectations so that they can devote themselves to and continually sharpen their expertise in Scripture. Likewise, those under the care of their ministry need the freedom to become hearers of the word without being saddled each week with the pastor's hobbyhorses and personal agendas. All in Christ's church can benefit from understanding what it means for a minister to be an approved workman for the gospel, building on the foundation of Christ.

The Work of the Approved Workman

Paul tells Timothy in 2 Timothy 2:15: "Be diligent to present yourself approved to God, a worker who does not need to be ashamed, rightly dividing the word of truth." The words "be diligent" communicate the idea of doing something with meticulousness, urgency, and zeal. Timothy is to devote himself earnestly to the approval of God rather than men. In no way is Paul implying that Timothy is to work for God's favor or earn the righteousness that God requires of every human being, for such blessing is possible only through Christ alone, as Paul makes abundantly clear (2 Tim. 1:9–10; cf. Rom. 3:21–26; 4:1–8; 5:1–2; Gal. 3:10–14; Eph. 2:8–9; Phil. 3:7–9). Rather, Paul means that Timothy is to labor for God's glory, not his own. As Paul reminded the Corinthians, "Not he who commends himself is approved, but whom the Lord commends" (2 Cor. 10:18).

Like similar statements in Paul's first letter to Timothy (e.g., 1 Tim. 1:18–19; 4:6–8, 13–15; 6:11–14), this verse makes a sharp contrast between the work of a faithful minister and that of false teachers. Whereas the latter ultimately seek the admiration of men, Timothy is to aim for the approval of God. The apostle develops this concept by the description "a worker who does not need to be ashamed." Shameful pandering for man's approval was a common trait among the false teachers and remains a temptation for every minister of the word. As Paul points out later in his letter, many people have "itching ears" and want to accumulate for themselves teachers who suit their own passions (4:3). Consequently, the minister of the word is often tempted to win the approval of the congregation by preaching what they want to hear rather than preaching what God has clearly said in His word. The pastor can also feel pressure to think up new and exciting ways to communicate the word and to remain on the cutting edge of popular topics in the culture or else suffer the reputation of being irrelevant and boring. But accommodating the itching ears of individuals is not the business of the faithful preacher of the gospel. "The preacher's business," says R. L. Dabney, "is to take what is given to him in the Scriptures, as it is given to him, and to endeavor to imprint it on the souls of men. All else is God's work."[1]

1. R. L. Dabney, *Evangelical Eloquence* (1870; repr., Edinburgh: Banner of Truth, 1999), 37.

Preaching and teaching for the glory of God rather than the approval of man require the minister to handle the "word of truth" rightly. The verb Paul uses in 2:15 for "rightly dividing" (*orthotomeo*) is rather peculiar. This is the only time it appears in the New Testament. The word means to "cut straight." It communicates the idea of a carpenter who measures carefully and cuts straight lines. He must be skilled in his craft if he wants to build a sound structure. In the same way, Timothy is to be a skilled workman who is diligent and careful in handling the text of Scripture. If wood is the material with which carpenters work and marble is that of sculptors, the text of Scripture is the material with which the minister works. He is to be faithful and accurate in his explanation and application of the text, for it is God's "word of truth" (2:15).

Fundamental to the workman's ability to rightly handle the word of truth is his ability to distinguish between law and gospel when interpreting and preaching a text. This distinction was a major component of the Reformation's approach to understanding the Bible. As Zacharias Ursinus says in his Larger Catechism 36, the law "requires our perfect obedience to God" and "promises eternal life to those who keep it," whereas the gospel "shows us the fulfillment in Christ of the righteousness that the law requires" and "promises eternal life freely because of Christ to those who believe in him."[2] In the gospel, God provides to us in Christ what He demands from us in the law. The law says, "Do this and live," but the gospel says, "Christ did it for you." John Calvin's successor in Geneva, Theodore Beza, said that the "ignorance of this distinction between law and gospel is one of the principal sources of the abuses which corrupted and still corrupt Christianity."[3] William Perkins, the father of Elizabethan Puritanism, urged new preachers to learn and use what he called the basic principle in application, which is the law-gospel

---

2. Zacharias Ursinus, Larger Catechism, in *An Introduction to the Heidelberg Catechism: Sources, History, and Theology*, ed. Lyle D. Bierma (Grand Rapids: Baker Academic, 2005), 168–69.

3. Theodore Beza, *The Christian Faith*, trans. James Clark (Lewes, England: Christian Focus, 1992), 41.

distinction. "The basic principle in application is to know whether the passage is a statement of the law or the gospel. For when the Word is preached, the law and the gospel operate differently. The law exposes the disease of sin, and as a side-effect stimulates and stirs it up. But it provides no remedy for it.... The law is, therefore, first in the order of teaching; then comes the gospel."[4] Perkins believed that it is a mishandling of the word of God to preach the law without making this critical distinction, for doing so will only confuse law and gospel and consequently rob Christ's sheep of the one thing that offers them hope in this life and motivates them to joyful, godly living.

Knowing how to rightly divide between law and gospel is not the only thing a faithful minister must do. His work requires him to be properly trained in the disciplines of hermeneutics (the art and science of interpreting texts) and exegesis (the critical explanation of a text). He must be proficient and tested in his abilities to read and interpret sacred Scripture in its original languages. We should no sooner sit under a minister who has no formal training in Greek and Hebrew than we should go to a doctor who has no formal training in medicine. If he is to present himself to God as an approved workman who has no need to be ashamed, he must be an expert in the word of God, for the word of God is the material with which he works.

Moreover, the minister must be educated in biblical and systematic theology, church history, apologetics, and homiletics. As Paul told Titus, a minister must hold fast "the faithful word as he has been taught, that he may be able, by sound doctrine, both to exhort and convict those who contradict" (Titus 1:9). He needs to be able to discern the difference between doctrine that is worth defending and mere quarrels about words, which do no good (v. 14).

The minister must also be examined by an ecclesiastical body of elders and ministers who are able to confirm his calling. It is

---

4. William Perkins, *The Art of Prophesying* (1592; repr., Edinburgh: Banner of Truth, 1996), 54.

not enough that a man senses the inward call to the ministry. If he is truly called by God to preach the word and shepherd souls, his inward call will be confirmed by an outward call from Christ's church. The New Testament knows nothing of men who appoint themselves to be pastors.

The minister's diligence to present himself approved, however, is not limited to seminary study and ordination exams. The faithful pastor is a perpetual student of the Bible, giving himself to rigorous study, regardless of the pressures and pace of daily life. Apart from this, he will not be strengthened in his abilities and never truly "be able to teach others also" (2 Tim. 2:2). As Thomas Murphy said in his classic *Pastoral Theology*, "The pastor must study, study, study, or he will not grow, or even live, as a true workman for Christ." He continues,

> It should be firmly settled by every pastor that close study is to be one great business of his whole life.... That his life is to be one of incessant study, he should fix upon as a fact from which there is to be no escaping if he would serve God in the gospel.... His study is not to be as a mere preparation for the ministry, to be dropped, or even remitted, when its active duties are entered upon, but is to be the incessant occupation of his life. It is not to be relaxed with years, but to go on filling and enriching the mind upon whose stores there will be such incessant draughts.[5]

Even Paul, after some thirty years of apostolic ministry and near the end of his life, did not outgrow his need to study. His urging Timothy to bring "the books, especially the parchments" (2 Tim. 4:13) is proof of that. As Calvin noted, "It is evident from this, that the Apostle had not given up reading, though he was already preparing for death. Where are those who think that they have made so great progress that they do not need any more exercise?"[6] If a man is

5. Thomas Murphy, *Pastoral Theology: The Pastor in the Various Duties of His Office* (1877; repr., Primedia eLaunch, 2013), 46.

6. Calvin, *Calvin's Commentaries*, vol. 21, 266.

not inclined to study the Scriptures diligently, he should stay out of the ministry. What the people of God need most is not the pastor's winsome personality or his dynamic presence, but the faithful and consistent preaching of Christ and Him crucified.

The Work of the Unapproved Workmen

As a wise and concerned mentor, Paul tells Timothy, "Shun profane and idle babblings" (2 Tim. 2:16a). The imperative verb in this sentence is in the present tense, characterizing the action as something Timothy must constantly do. This responsibility is part of his broader obligation to guard the good deposit entrusted to him (1:14). It connects to Paul's warning in 2:14: "Remind them of these things, charging them before the Lord not to strive about words to no profit, to the ruin of the hearers." The false teachers promoting heresy in Ephesus were substituting "the word of truth" (2:15) for what Paul calls a quarrel about words, which does no good (2:14).

Not all theological debates are bad. In fact, we are commanded "to contend earnestly for the faith" when necessary (Jude 3; cf. Gal. 2:11–14; 1 Tim. 6:12). But debates that turn into quarrels are rarely fruitful, and quarrels that take our focus off of Christ and the essentials of the historic Christian faith never do good. In our day of online theological debates, we would do well to remember this important point. The internet has no shortage of online warriors who seem to thrive on arguing over the slightest nuances of Scripture. Some, filled with digital courage, rashly condemn their opponents as heretics without any due process in an ecclesiastical assembly. How many of these Twitter storms and Facebook wars are little more than unprofitable quarrels? Not all theological debates are alike. Those that are truly worthy of our engagement are the ones in which there is a clear attack on the Christian faith as summarized in the ancient creeds and the confessions of the Protestant Reformation. Such false teaching is what Paul calls "idle babblings," or, it could be translated, "empty chatter."

The apostle states two reasons for eschewing this empty chatter: "for they will increase to more ungodliness. And their message will spread like cancer" (2:16b–17a). Whereas "rightly dividing the word of truth" (2:15) produces godliness in those who respond to it in faith, the word of the false teachers "will increase to more ungodliness." Their irreverent babble ultimately leads a person away from Christ and to destruction. If the false teaching is tolerated rather than avoided and stopped, it will continue to spread in the body of Christ like an aggressive cancer.

For this reason, Paul, in both his first and second letters to Timothy, warned his younger colleague about the false doctrine that was advancing in the city and making shipwreck of the faith for some (1 Tim. 1:19).[7] This heresy included the claim that "the resurrection is already past" (2 Tim. 2:18). Being a good shepherd who wanted to protect Christ's flock, Paul was not afraid to name names. Hymenaeus and Philetus were two men "who have strayed concerning the truth, saying that the resurrection is already past" (2:18). The verb that Paul uses for "strayed" (*astocheo*) comes from a Greek noun meaning "target" (*stochos*). Paul uses it to describe the heretics missing the mark in their teaching, deviating from orthodoxy.[8] George Knight explains, "It was probably associated with a false asceticism and a low view of the material world, especially of the human body, and might have resulted from an incorrect handling of Paul's words about Christians being presently raised with Christ (Rom. 6:1–11; Eph. 2:6; 5:14; Col. 2:12, 13; 3:1–4)."[9]

To put it another way, this heresy conflated the "already" with the "not yet." Believers are *already* raised with Christ in the sense that they have been raised from spiritual death, are united with Him, and indwelt by the Holy Spirit (Rom. 6:3–8; 8:9–10; Eph. 1:13–14; 2:1–6; Col. 2:12; 3:1–3). But they are *not yet* raised from the dead physically. The resurrection of the body is a real event in

7. For further details about the false teaching circulating in Ephesus, see the introduction.

8. The same verb is used in 1 Timothy 6:21 where Paul describes those who profess "the profane and idle babblings and contradictions of what is falsely called knowledge" (v. 20) as having "strayed concerning the faith."

9. Knight, *Pastoral Epistles*, 414.

the future that will mark the completion of our salvation on the day of Christ's return (Rom. 8:23–25; 1 Cor. 15:20–57; 2 Cor. 5:1–5; Phil. 3:20–21; Col. 3:4). As those already justified and united to Christ, we presently participate partially in the age to come. But we are still being sanctified and have not yet been glorified. This is why the Christian church confesses in the Nicene Creed, "I look for the resurrection of the dead, and the life of the world to come." The notion that the resurrection of the body has already happened is a direct assault on the historic Christian faith. It undermines the hope of believers (2 Tim. 4:18; cf. 1 Tim. 1:19; 6:20–21) and disrupts their faith (2 Tim. 2:18).

Paul's conflict with Hymenaeus and Philetus was not a minor disagreement. Their teaching represented a direct attack on a critical doctrine of Christianity. The apostle was not being uncharitable or unreasonably harsh by naming Hymenaeus and Philetus, for they were unapproved workmen, building on an unstable foundation.

The Foundation on Which the Workman Builds

Second Timothy 2:19 provides us with hope and encouragement: "Nevertheless the solid foundation of God stands," says Paul. He emphasizes the immovable character of truth. Truth belongs to God, and it does not change. This is a glaring contrast to the deviant claims of the false teachers, which were built on an entirely different foundation altogether.

The true foundation, on the other hand, bears "this seal: 'The Lord knows those who are His,' and, 'Let everyone who names the name of Christ depart from iniquity.'" Seals were used in the ancient world to identify proper ownership, whether in the form of soft wax on scrolls or inscriptions on structures. Paul seems to have in mind the latter in this case. The true foundation, on which the structure is built, bears a seal with a dual truth that counters the claims of the false teachers. "The Lord knows those who are His" seems to be a quotation from Numbers 16:5 about the Lord's judgment of Korah, a man who rose up against Moses. Just as God protected the foundation of His truth during the days of that opponent, so too would

He do the same regarding those who opposed Paul and Timothy. "Let everyone who names the name of Christ depart from iniquity" seems also to draw from this scene in Numbers 16, which describes the separation of faithful Israelites from the iniquity of Korah and his followers (vv. 26–27), who were about to be judged by God.

It is important for us to note Paul's use of architectural imagery ("the solid foundation of God") in verse 19. The New Testament often employs such metaphors to describe the church. For example, in 1 Corinthians 3:10–11 Paul says, "According to the grace of God which was given to me, as a wise master builder I have laid the foundation, and another builds on it. But let each one take heed how he builds on it. For no other foundation can anyone lay than that which is laid, which is Jesus Christ." And in Ephesians 2:19–22, we read that believers are "fellow citizens with the saints and members of the household of God, having been built on the foundation of the apostles and prophets, Jesus Christ Himself being the chief cornerstone, in whom the whole building, being fitted together, grows into a holy temple in the Lord, in whom you also are being built together for a dwelling place of God in the Spirit." These passages are ultimately fulfillments of God's promise to David in the Old Testament that his Son would build a house that would stand forever (see 2 Sam. 7:1–17). One from David's line would establish the true temple and house of God and sit on David's throne forever. Of his kingdom there would be no end.

That person, of course, is Jesus Christ, who came in the fullness of time to fulfill the Davidic covenant by building a house for God's name (Luke 1:32–33; cf. Isa. 28:16). The house He constructed was not built with wood and stone, but with living people (1 Cor. 6:19; 1 Peter 2:5). He built this temple-house by living a perfect life of righteousness, dying an atoning death on the cross, and being raised again from the dead gloriously. His blood purged our sins, His righteousness has been imputed to us, and He has sent the Holy Spirit to indwell us, making us the temple of the living God.

In one sense, Christ is the true workman "who does not need to be ashamed," for He has promised, "I will build My church, and the gates of Hades shall not prevail against it" (Matt. 16:18b). Christ is the Master Builder, and the kingdom He builds cannot be shaken (Heb. 12:25–28). If the United States were to come under nuclear attack or if its economy were to collapse, the kingdom that Christ builds would not be affected, for its foundations are eternal.

Yet the Master Builder is also pleased to call workmen to labor diligently under His care. He wants His workmen to build on no other foundation but that which He has already laid. Through their faithful labor, Christ is building us up together as "a spiritual house" (1 Peter 2:5). Through the means of God's ordained craftsmanship—namely, His word and sacraments—the Master Builder is bringing you to completion. You will not end up like Michelangelo's *Rondanini Pietà*, an unfinished and incomplete work, for "He who has begun a good work in you will complete it until the day of Jesus Christ" (Phil. 1:6).

Let us be grateful, therefore, for ministers who preach the word faithfully. Let us pray for them, asking God to grant them grace to be workmen who have no need to be ashamed but who labor in the Scriptures diligently, "rightly dividing the word of truth."

8

Vessels of Honor

2 TIMOTHY 2:20–26

But in a great house there are not only vessels of gold and silver, but also of wood and clay, some for honor and some for dishonor. Therefore if anyone cleanses himself from the latter, he will be a vessel for honor, sanctified and useful for the Master, prepared for every good work. Flee also youthful lusts; but pursue righteousness, faith, love, peace with those who call on the Lord out of a pure heart. But avoid foolish and ignorant disputes, knowing that they generate strife. And a servant of the Lord must not quarrel but be gentle to all, able to teach, patient, in humility correcting those who are in opposition, if God perhaps will grant them repentance, so that they may know the truth, and that they may come to their senses and escape the snare of the devil, having been taken captive by him to do his will.

So far in his second letter to Timothy, Paul has used four metaphors to describe the faithful pastor. He must be a loyal soldier (2:3), a self-disciplined athlete (2:5), a hardworking farmer (2:6), and a skilled workman (2:15). The minister of the word must strive to be all of these things in his service to Christ and His church. Now, in 2:20–21, Paul adds a fifth image to fill out his portrait of the faithful minister: he must be an honorable vessel in the household of God.

Vessels of Honor

The word that Paul uses for "vessel" (*skeuos*) means "instrument." It is the same word used by the Lord in Acts 9:15, where He calls

Paul "a chosen vessel of Mine." Used in the context of Paul's analogy, the word evokes the idea of a household instrument designed for a specific use. Think of how a kitchen is equipped with a variety of pots, pans, and utensils, each one intended for a particular purpose. If you want to make a frittata, you reach for a skillet, not a stock-pot. But if you want to make minestrone, it's the other way around. And if you want to eat the frittata, you use a fork. But a fork is the wrong utensil for eating minestrone. There are different vessels for different needs.

In the ancient world, a large house owned by a wealthy person would have a wide range of utensils, everything from gold and silver dinnerware to wood and clay toilets. Some vessels were "for honor and some for dishonor" (2:20). The apostle uses this analogy in order to juxtapose two different types of teachers within the household of God. The "great house" of which he speaks is the visible church on earth (e.g. Gal. 6:10; Eph. 2:19–20). The visible church is a mixture of true believers and hypocrites, faithful teachers and false teachers.

When Protestants speak of the distinction between the visible and invisible church, it is not without good reason. We make this distinction because we recognize Scripture's clear portrayal of the church as both the elect people of God, whose names are written in the Lamb's Book of Life (Rev. 21:27), and the visible community of faith established on earth (Matt. 28:18–20). Yet, as Scripture also shows us, these two are not always one and the same. There is the church as we see it and the church as God sees it. What is discernible to us with the physical eye is not the same as what is known to God in His omniscience. Protestants, therefore, have included specific language in their confessions to uphold this important distinction as part of their ecclesiology. In the Reformed churches, for example, we confess in article 29 of the Belgic Confession that there are "hypocrites, who are mixed in the church along with the good and yet are not part of the church, although they are outwardly in it." Likewise, chapter 25 of the Westminster Confession of Faith points out that "the catholic or universal Church which is invisible consists of the whole number of the elect" and that "the visible Church...consists of all those throughout the world that profess the true religion and of their children."

As a minister in the household of God, Timothy was to make it his aim to be an honorable vessel. "Therefore if anyone cleanses himself from the latter, he will be a vessel for honor, sanctified and useful for the Master, prepared for every good work" (2:21). The translators for the New King James Version wisely inserted a comma after the word "honor" because everything that follows in the sentence is an appositional statement, explaining in three terms what it means for a minister to cleanse himself from that which is dishonorable.

First, he must be "sanctified"—that is, set apart as holy. Every believer is made holy by virtue of the imputed righteousness of Christ, which is received through faith alone. Paul's emphasis in this verse, however, is not about the way in which a sinner is cleansed and made holy but about the consecration of a minister in his office. At his ordination, hands are laid on him by the elders, and he is set apart in devotion to prayer and to the ministry of the word (cf. Acts 6:4; Eph. 4:11–12; 2 Tim. 4:2–5). His vocation is holy. He must therefore conduct himself in a manner worthy of his calling. This does not apply only to his godliness of life but also to his doctrine. Timothy must keep himself pure from dishonorable doctrine and remain set apart from false teachers like Hymenaeus and Philetus (2 Tim. 2:17–18).

Second, the minister must be "useful for the Master." The title *minister* means "servant." He is not a king, CEO, or boss, but a servant of the church of Jesus Christ. His usefulness to the Master is not determined by the size of his church, the popularity of his name, or the crowds he commands as a conference speaker but by his faithfulness in service, no matter how unspectacular and ordinary it may appear before the world. He is a servant of the Master, called to feed and care for the household of God. He must therefore cleanse himself from what is dishonorable.

Third, he must be "prepared for every good work." The emphasis in this phrase falls on the readiness of the minister more than the actual good works themselves. In other words, keeping a close watch on himself and on his teaching (1 Tim. 4:16; cf. Acts 20:28) allows the minister to maintain a proper state of readiness for his service.

Like the metaphors of soldier, athlete, and farmer, the metaphor of an honorable vessel has a broader application to all believers, not just ministers. If you are a Christian, God has given you particular gifts and abilities to be used for the benefit of others. You are an instrument in His hands. Each of us has a role to play within the body of Christ (Rom. 12:4–6; 1 Cor. 12:12–27; Eph. 4:4, 16). As the Heidelberg Catechism 55 explains, to participate in the communion of saints means that "believers, one and all, as members of the Lord Jesus Christ, are partakers with him in all his treasures and gifts" and "that each one must feel himself bound to use his gifts readily and cheerfully for the advantage and welfare of other members." To be an instrument useful to the Master of the house and ready for every good work, we must cleanse ourselves from what is dishonorable. As those who have been cleansed by the blood of Christ and clothed in His righteousness, we are now called to present our bodies "a living sacrifice, holy, acceptable to God," not being "conformed to this world," but "transformed by the renewing of your mind" (Rom. 12:1–2). In other words, be who you are! Because you have a new identity in Christ, live accordingly, as an honorable vessel in service to the Master, prepared for good works (Gal. 6:10; Eph. 2:10; Col. 1:10).

Fleeing and Pursuing

A natural part of cleansing oneself from what is dishonorable is fleeing sin and pursuing holiness. "Flee also youthful lusts," Paul tells Timothy in 2:22. The verb he uses for "flee" (*pheugo*) is the same verb used by the angel who told Joseph in a dream to "flee to Egypt" (Matt. 2:13) and by Stephen when he described Moses fleeing from Pharaoh (Acts 7:29). The verb is used to show the action of one fleeing from physical harm. It is with this same sense of urgency that Christians are called to flee sin and spiritual danger (1 Cor. 6:18; 10:14). "We are to recognize sin as something dangerous to the soul," warned John Stott. "We are not to come to terms with it, or even negotiate with it. We are not to linger in its presence like Lot in Sodom. On the contrary we are to get as far away as possible as quickly as possible. Like Joseph, when Potiphar's wife attempted to seduce him, we are to take to our heels and run."[1]

If you find it difficult "to take to your heels and run" from sin and youthful passions, remember two things: First, *sin is not your friend.* At times we find it tempting to be friendly with various forms of sin, for sin seems to promise us joy and fulfillment. It offers us a temporary thrill, making us feel alive and exhilarated. It tells us that we can have a brief escape from the daily grind and pressures of life. But sin never has our best interest in mind. It is a false friend, wanting only to abuse, rule, and destroy us. Sin is waiting to stab us in the back and then laugh at us when we are humiliated and ashamed. As John Owen warned in his seventeenth-century classic *The Mortification of Sin in Believers*, sin is never satisfied with how much space we allow it to occupy in our lives. It always wants more. He explained,

> Sin will not only be striving, acting, rebelling, troubling, disquieting, but if left alone, if not continually mortified, it brings forth great, cursed, scandalous, soul-destroying sins.... Sin aims always at the utmost; every time it rises up to tempt or entice, might it have its own course, it would go out to the utmost sin in that kind. Every unclean thought or glance would be adultery if it could; every covetous desire would be oppression, every thought of unbelief would be atheism, might it grow to its head.... Every rise of lust, might it have its course, would come to the height of villainy: it is like the grave that is never satisfied.[2]

Sin is not your friend. Whatever it promises you is only a lie. In reality sin is an aggressive enemy that wants to destroy marriages, ruin families, divide friends, and split churches. Flee from it!

---

1. Stott, *Message of 2 Timothy*, 74.

2. John Owen, *The Mortification of Sin in Believers*, in *The Works of John Owen*, ed. William H. Goold (Edinburgh: T&T Clark, 1862), 6:12.

The second thing to remember is this: if you are in Christ, *sin is not your master*. You do not have to obey it like a slave, for Christ Jesus has set you free. Jesus said, "Whoever commits sin is a slave of sin. And a slave does not abide in the house forever, but a son abides forever. Therefore if the Son makes you free, you shall be free indeed" (John 8:34–36). Through His life, death, and resurrection, Christ delivered His people not only from the penalty of sin but also from the power of sin. Although the believer is engaged in a lifelong struggle against sin, he or she is no longer ruled by sin. "But God be thanked that though you were slaves of sin, yet you obeyed from the heart that form of doctrine to which you were delivered. And having been set free from sin, you become slaves of righteousness" (Rom. 6:17–18). You are indwelled by the Holy Spirit, who is the down payment of the inheritance that your Lord purchased for you. Sin is not your master, Christ is.

Paul tells Timothy not only to flee from sin but also to pursue holiness: "Flee also youthful lusts; but pursue righteousness, faith, love, peace with those who call on the Lord out of a pure heart" (2:22). Just as we are to run away from spiritual danger, we are also to run toward spiritual health. This is not the first time Paul has used the imagery of fleeing and pursuing when exhorting his beloved colleague. In 1 Timothy 6:11, the apostle tells the young pastor to flee false teaching and the love of money (referring to his previous remarks in verses 3–10) and "pursue righteousness, godliness, faith, love, patience, gentleness." Some of these same virtues make his list in 2 Timothy.

Pursuing "righteousness, faith, love, [and] peace" requires ministers to pursue Christ in His word not only for those whom they serve but also for themselves. Thomas Murphy explains: "Those who are appointed to feed others in the green pastures—should they not themselves know well where and what those pastures are? Those who are to lead others in the paths of righteousness should themselves be familiar with those paths. Those who would guard others from straying must surely be themselves well-fortified by the strength and the watchfulness that come from the Omnipotent Spirit!"[3]

Pursuing Christ in His word is not a mere intellectual exercise. The pastor must seek to be a man of "righteousness, faith, love, and peace," an honorable vessel in matters of life. In other words, he must be a man of godly character. Nowadays, in our pragmatic culture, character seems to count for so little. If a man can turn a profit for the company or has a sound economic plan for the nation, it doesn't really matter if he is a person of high moral quality. So goes the thinking of the world. But when it comes to the qualifications for leaders in Christ's church, the Bible is very clear that character matters. A minister must be a man not only of skill and ability but also above reproach, faithful to his wife, sober-minded, self-controlled, and respectable. He must be an honorable vessel.

Be Kind to Everyone, Patiently Enduring Evil

When we think of youthful lusts from which Christians should flee, perhaps the first thing that comes to mind is sins of sexual immorality and lust. Indeed, these are deadly, life-destroying evils for which every Christian must be on guard, especially today, when pornography is so easily accessible on our computers and phones. Ministers in particular, regardless of their age, must be ever vigilant against these youthful passions. How many churches have suffered, ministries have been destroyed, and families have been ripped apart because of a pastor who committed adultery? "Let him who thinks he stands take heed lest he fall" (1 Cor. 10:12).

The "youthful lusts" to which Paul refers in 2:22, however, are not limited to sexual immorality. In fact, his emphasis is on sins of another kind to which ministers, especially young ones like Timothy, can be particularly susceptible: pride, impatience, and anger. These sins can be perilous to an effective ministry and threaten the peace of the church. Most men who enter the ministry do so because they love Christ and want to help people, not hurt them.

3. Murphy, *Pastoral Theology*, 17.

But if a man's pride and anger are not kept in constant check, hurting Christ's beloved sheep becomes a real risk, even if the minister is a faithful preacher of the gospel. Pastors who are determined to win unnecessary arguments and insist on getting their own way in the church are in great danger of doing damage to all the good that they have done.

For this reason, Paul warns Timothy not to die on every hill. "But avoid foolish and ignorant disputes, knowing that they generate strife" (2:23). The Greek word for "disputes" (*zetesis*) is used in this context to mean an unprofitable and foolish debate. It is used in the same way in 1 Timothy 6:4 and Titus 3:9. It is a useless speculation that only breeds unhealthy arguments.

This is not a prohibition on all theological debate. The New Testament commands us to "contend earnestly for the faith which was once for all delivered to the saints" (Jude 3). When the gospel was at stake, Paul himself opposed Peter "to his face" (Gal. 2:11–14). Likewise, Timothy was under obligation to "fight the good fight of faith" (1 Tim. 6:12) and guard the good deposit entrusted to him (2 Tim. 1:14). What God forbids, however, is quarreling over speculations, nonessential doctrines, and matters of little importance. Such controversies are futile and only stir up strife. How many times has a church leadership meeting become contentious because of arguments over mundane matters such as the color of the carpet or the purchase of a new air-conditioning unit? How often do ministers behave in a manner unbecoming of their office while furiously debating someone on Facebook or Twitter? How frequently do our pride and sense of self-importance get the best of us because we were annoyed with someone? Paul warns Timothy to choose his battles wisely.

He also warns him to watch his tone at all times: "And a servant of the Lord must not quarrel but be gentle to all, able to teach, patient, in humility correcting those who are in opposition" (2:24–25a). The Christian minister must not only be "able to teach" (cf. 1 Tim. 3:2), possessing spiritual gifts and undergoing adequate training for interpreting, proclaiming, and explaining the word of

God clearly, he must seek to be meek. Gentleness is becoming of the servant of the Lord, for he is called to be like his Master. The apostle Peter says,

> For to this you were called, because Christ also suffered for us, leaving us an example, that you should follow His steps:
>
> "Who committed no sin,
> Nor was deceit found in His mouth";
>
> who, when He was reviled, did not revile in return; when He suffered, He did not threaten, but committed Himself to Him who judges righteously. (1 Peter 2:21–23)

As a representative of Christ, the Christian minister must strive to put on "the meekness and gentleness of Christ" (2 Cor. 10:1). Angry words and a harsh tone are out of place.

Far too often, though, we wrongly assume that our anger is righteous, as if our quarreling has the same moral quality as the holy indignation of Jesus when He cleansed the temple or rebuked the Pharisees. The difference between righteous anger and sinful anger, however, is that the former focuses on God and His kingdom, rights, and concerns; and the latter focuses on me and my kingdom, rights, and concerns.[4] "Righteous anger," says Robert Jones, "focuses on how people offend God and his name, not me and my name.... Righteous anger remains self-controlled. It keeps its head without cursing, screaming, raging, or flying off the handle. Nor does it spiral downward in self-pity or despair. It does not ignore people, snub people, or withdraw from people."[5] If you find that you are struggling with anger, ask yourself why you are angry. Are you ignoring someone, snubbing someone, or withdrawing from someone because of what that person did to you? Are you angry with that person because of how he dishonored God, or because your pride has been

4. See Robert D. Jones, *Uprooting Anger: Biblical Help for a Common Problem* (Phillipsburg, N.J.: P&R, 2005), 29.

5. Jones, *Uprooting Anger*, 29.

hurt? "Righteous anger arises because of the other person's sin against God, not because of your personal hurts or vengeful desires."[6]

James reminds us that anger is not something we have, but something we do. Whatever provoked our anger was not the root cause. Rather, the cause of our anger lies in our sinful hearts. "Where do wars and fights come from among you? Do they not come from your desires for pleasure that war in your members?" (James 4:1). Anger arises from the desires that dominate our heart. It manifests itself when our idols are threatened and we don't get what we want so desperately: to look good in front of others, be esteemed by our peers, keep up appearances, or win an argument. This is especially challenging when we receive unfair criticism. Driven to make ourselves look better, we conjure up our inner lawyer and respond to unfair criticism with proud, sharp, and defensive words. The early church father John Chrysostom reminds us, "Let us not use anger as an excuse, but let us talk with them gently and with kindness. Nothing is more forceful and effective than treatment which is gentle and kind."[7]

But what if we believe the person with whom we are angry has truly sinned against us? Does that justify our anger? The truth is that how we respond when we think someone has sinned against us often reveals our self-righteousness. It is easy for us to appoint ourselves as prosecutor, judge, and jury of the accused and assume an air of moral superiority, as if we ourselves are incapable of the sin committed against us. Telling ourselves that our anger is righteous so that we feel justified, we inevitably wage war against God's mercy.

Yet there is good news for self-righteous, judgmental, and angry people: Christ's mercy triumphs over my self-righteous judgment (James 2:13). When I recognize afresh the grace and mercy of God extended to me through the finished work of Jesus Christ, I am reawakened to the bankruptcy of my own righteousness. Like

---

6. Jones, *Uprooting Anger*, 40.

7. John Chrysostom, *On the Incomprehensible Nature of God*, 1.7, in *Ancient Christian Commentary on Scripture*, 256.

smelling salts that revive me from my self-righteous stupor, the grace and mercy of God send me running to Christ for His righteousness. Only there, in the gospel, can we find the strength to be "gentle to all," patiently enduring evil (2 Tim. 2:24).

Repentance Leading to Knowledge of the Truth

The Christian minister must also be kind to those who are openly hostile to the gospel. He must patiently endure evil and correct opponents of the faith with gentleness. For, as Paul explains, "God perhaps will grant them repentance, so that they may know the truth, and that they may come to their senses and escape the snare of the devil, having been taken captive by him to do his will" (2:25b–26). God alone grants repentance. Only the Holy Spirit can illumine the mind and regenerate the heart, liberating the captive soul from Satan.[8] Coming to their senses and confessing the truth is a consequence of the repentance granted by the irresistible grace of God.

No one is beyond the reach of God's grace in Christ, not even the great persecutor of the early church, Saul of Tarsus. Remembering this important truth, we must treat everyone—even the most hardened and belligerent pagan—as potentially numbered among God's elect. John Calvin explains,

> Since the conversion of a man is in the hand of God, who knows whether they who today appear to be unteachable shall be suddenly changed by the power of God, into other men? Thus, whoever shall consider that repentance is the gift and work of God, will cherish more earnest hope, and, encouraged by this confidence, will bestow more toil and exertion for the instruction of rebels. We should view it thus, that our duty is,

---

8. There has been considerable debate surrounding the meaning of two pronouns in the concluding words "having been taken captive by him to do his will." Some have interpreted both pronouns to refer to God ("having been taken captive by him [God] to do his [God's] will"), while others have taken this to mean "having been taken captive by the devil to do God's will." Most scholars, however, read the pronouns to refer to the devil. For excellent defenses of this position, see Knight, *Pastoral Epistles*, 425–27; and Stott, *Message of 2 Timothy*, 79–80.

> to be employed in sowing and watering, and, while we do this, we must look for the increase from God.[9]

Far from causing us to be lazy in our evangelism or indifferent toward the lost, the doctrines of grace move us to be like Christ, who had compassion for sinners.

Looking at the passage of 2:20–26 as a whole, we can see that Christlikeness is ultimately the moral quality Paul tells Timothy to cultivate. Jesus Himself is the perfect example of righteousness, love, peace, kindness, patience, and gentleness. If those who proclaim Christ desire to be "sanctified and useful for the Master, prepared for every good work" (2:21), they must cleanse themselves from what is dishonorable and pursue Christlikeness.

Once again, we are reminded that no man is sufficient for these things, which is why the minister must "be strong in the grace that is in Christ Jesus" (2:1). There is no such thing as a perfect pastor, a man who is so holy that he has outgrown his need to cleanse himself constantly from what is dishonorable and pursue daily the virtues of righteousness, faith, love, and peace. That is why Paul tells Timothy to pursue these things; it is a constant chase and daily struggle.

Ministers and elders: remember that you must never stop pursuing Christlikeness. God has called you to be honorable vessels in the household of God and an example to others. On the one hand, do not use your passion for the truth, your fiery personality, or your sinfulness as excuses for your angry words, harsh tone, and impatience. As one writer put it, "Holding the right position in the argument never justifies betraying the character of Jesus."[10] On the other hand, if you are a person who is prone to passivity, people pleasing, and avoiding confrontation, do not use an appeal to gentleness, kindness, and patience to justify your fear of man. Jesus was none of these things. Neither extreme is what Paul describes as an honorable vessel. Therefore, confess your sins and ask for

---

9. Calvin, *Calvin's Commentaries*, vol. 21, 234.

10. Zack Eswine, *The Imperfect Pastor* (Wheaton, Ill.: Crossway, 2015), 239.

forgiveness. Continue fighting the good fight not only in doctrine but also in life. Keep running your race with endurance, looking always to the Lord Jesus, "the author and finisher of our faith, who for the joy that was set before Him endured the cross, despising the shame, and has sat down at the right hand of the throne of God" (Heb. 12:2). Look to Him, trust in Him, and draw near to Him!

Christian, remember that like you, leaders in the church are still in the process of being sanctified. Perhaps you are disappointed with your pastor because he is not as patient and gentle as you would like him to be. Maybe he has let you down in the past not because of what he said but because of how he said it. Perhaps in your struggle to forgive him, you have become so preoccupied with his flaws, faults, and shortcomings that you are having a hard time receiving the means of grace from him. You must remember that your pastor is imperfect and has not yet arrived at complete "righteousness, faith, love, peace" (2 Tim. 2:22). Like you, he is called to pursue those virtues. At times he will need godly correction from the elders. If he refuses to repent or has committed sin worthy of public discipline, he must be held accountable by the ecclesiastical body to whom he submits. Your responsibility, however, is not to be his judge or to gossip about him, but to pray for him in his weaknesses, honor his office (1 Tim. 5:17), and submit to him, for he, with the elders, has been appointed to keep watch over your soul as a servant who will have to give an account to the Lord (Heb. 13:17). And pray for yourself. Be mindful of Satan's devices. The devil wants to snatch away from you the preached word like a bird devouring seed that falls on hardened soil. He wants you to stop looking to Jesus and instead look only at your pastor's failure to meet your personal expectations.

The good news for all who are in Christ is that God has granted us repentance leading to knowledge of the truth. Righteousness, faith, love, and peace are ours through the Lord Jesus. He has justified us and declared us righteous, by virtue of the righteousness of Christ. He has granted us the gift of faith, having regenerated our hearts by the Holy Spirit. He has given us a new disposition that loves God and loves our neighbor. We have peace with God through our Lord Jesus Christ, who, by His Spirit, is making us peacemakers. In Christ, the Spirit is at work in us, producing fruit to the glory of God. Therefore, let us all pursue Christlikeness with joy and gratitude, being strengthened by the grace that is in Christ Jesus.

9

Difficulty in the Last Days

2 TIMOTHY 3:1–9

But know this, that in the last days perilous times will come: For men will be lovers of themselves, lovers of money, boasters, proud, blasphemers, disobedient to parents, unthankful, unholy, unloving, unforgiving, slanderers, without self-control, brutal, despisers of good, traitors, headstrong, haughty, lovers of pleasure rather than lovers of God, having a form of godliness but denying its power. And from such people turn away! For of this sort are those who creep into households and make captives of gullible women loaded down with sins, led away by various lusts, always learning and never able to come to the knowledge of the truth. Now as Jannes and Jambres resisted Moses, so do these also resist the truth: men of corrupt minds, disapproved concerning the faith; but they will progress no further, for their folly will be manifest to all, as theirs also was.

"The conquering power of evil is on the increase. This is characteristic of the last times. Innocent babies are now not even allowed to be born, so corrupted are the moral standards. Or if born, no one educates them, so desolate are studies. Or if trained, no one enforces the training, so impotent are the laws. In fact, the case for modesty… has in our time become an obsolete subject."[1] Although these words could easily describe the moral erosion we see today in the modern Western world, they are in fact from the pen of Tertullian, an early church father who lived in Carthage in the Roman province

1. Tertullian, *On Modesty*, 7.1, in *Ancient Christian Commentary on Scripture*, 258–59.

of Africa during the late second and early third centuries. Like us, Tertullian lived in times of difficulty, when there was a noticeable decline in society's decency and virtue. Reading these comments helps us to remember that sin has been a perennial problem with humans ever since Adam rebelled in the garden. Godlessness is characteristic of every historical period. Never was there a golden age in which selfishness, greed, and violence were absent. We should avoid romanticizing the past, as if people were less sinful in days gone by. But we should also avoid romanticizing the future, as if the world is gradually healing from the catastrophic effects of the fall. We need a sober assessment of the problem of sin in society, especially if we are to appreciate the power of the gospel.

In 2 Timothy 3:1–9, the apostle Paul provides us with such an assessment. He wants to help Timothy put the difficulties he was facing into the context of what characterizes the last days. His young colleague should not be surprised by opposition from false teachers or by the rampant immorality in the city in which he served, for he lived in evil times, and the evil would only increase. Paul gives Timothy an accurate diagnosis of the radical corruption of the human heart so that he will put his confidence in God and His word, which alone is able to make one "wise for salvation through faith which is in Christ Jesus" (3:15b). Like a good soldier, disciplined athlete, and hardworking farmer (2:3–6), Timothy must stay focused and labor diligently in times of difficulty, preaching the word boldly in the midst of a crooked and twisted generation.

The church today needs that same confidence and focus. We are too easily tempted to look for external solutions to the pervasive problem of sin, as if more laws or better public policies could produce righteousness in the human heart. Paul's diagnosis of the last days in 3:1–9 not only helps us grasp the depths of societal depravity but also reminds us that only the gospel can regenerate the human heart and cause a sinner to live for the glory of God.

As we consider Paul's powerful description of the difficulty in the last days, let us think about the times in which we live, the trouble that is to come, and the word in which we trust.

The Times in Which We Live

"But know this, that in the last days perilous times will come" (3:1). When are "the last days"? Was Paul referring to a period that would take place in Timothy's time, or at the end of the age, immediately before the return of Christ? How do we know if we are living in the last days right now? According to the New Testament, the phrase "last days" is a reference to the whole period between Christ's first and second comings. In Acts 2:17, for example, the apostle Peter, while preaching at the Feast of Pentecost, quoted the prophet Joel, who said that "in the last days" God would pour out His Spirit on all flesh. Peter drew on this passage in order to explain that the outpouring of the Spirit in his time was a fulfillment of this prophecy. In other words, according to both the prophet Joel and the apostle Peter, the outpouring of the Holy Spirit was evidence that the last days had begun.

In similar fashion, the writer to the Hebrews begins his letter by saying, "God, who at various times and in various ways spoke in time past to the fathers by the prophets, has *in these last days* spoken to us by His Son" (vv. 1:1–2a; cf. James 5:3; 2 Peter 3:3). The last days were inaugurated when the incarnate Word came into the world. Everything from the time of creation until Christ's incarnation is ancient history. But with Christ's resurrection and ascension, history has entered its last lap and is moving closer to the finish line.

By "last days," then, Paul means his day as much as ours. As Augustine said during the early fifth century, "Indeed those last days were spoken of even in the first days of the apostles when the Lord's ascension into heaven was a recent happening.... So there were last days even then! How much more now is this so, even if there remained as many days to the end as have already passed from the ascension of the Lord to this day, or even if there remain more or less days to come!"[2]

2. Augustine, *Letters* 199.8.23–24, in *Ancient Christian Commentary on Scripture*, 259.

These last days are also "perilous" (*chalepos*). Paul uses a word that is found only one other time in the New Testament in Matthew 8:28 where it describes the condition of the demoniac in the Gadarenes whom Jesus healed. His violent and savage disposition was described with the same Greek word used in 3:1, which the New King James Version (NKJV) has translated as "perilous" and the English Standard Version (ESV) as "difficulty." This gives us an idea of the kind of evil the church faces until Christ's return. The times are evil, when "evil men and imposters will grow worse and worse, deceiving and being deceived" (3:13).

In one sense, perilous times are nothing new. One only has to read the Old Testament to see that godless societies have existed since the fall. Whether it was in the days of Noah or Israel's judges and apostate kings, times of difficulty are a perpetual challenge for God's people. Paul, however, is telling Timothy that something different is on the horizon. The perilous times that he describes will take place alongside the preaching of the gospel and the making of disciples. Although today is "the day of salvation" (2 Cor. 6:2) because Christ has accomplished redemption and God's judgment is delayed, it is also a day marked with difficulty, not ease. Christ's kingdom has already been inaugurated, but it has not yet been consummated. Satan has been bound so that he can no longer deceive the nations (Matt. 12:28–29; Rev. 20:1–3), but only in the sense that the gospel advances throughout the world to people of all nations (Matt. 28:18–20; Rev. 5:9; 7:9). During this period, Satan still "transforms himself into an angel of light" (2 Cor. 11:14) and brings difficulty and trouble to the people of God. As Jesus told His disciples, "These things I have spoken to you, that in Me you may have peace. In the world you will have tribulation; but be of good cheer, I have overcome the world" (John 16:33).

Looking back over the last several centuries, we can see a progression of evil in the way the world thinks about God and themselves. For example, for the first sixteen centuries after the ascension of Christ, as Christianity spread throughout the world, it was commonly understood that God's revelation stands above human reason. Theological debates typically centered on what God has said in His word, with everyone assuming that the Bible was the authoritative word of God. During the late seventeenth and early eighteenth centuries, however, a period known as modernity arose. New claims from Enlightenment philosophers popularized the belief that human reason stands above God's revelation, essentially reversing what was previously held to be true. This eventually changed the way most Westerners viewed the authority of Scripture. Higher criticism and skepticism began to increase. Debates shifted from what God has said in the Bible to the question of whether or not we can trust the Bible at all.

Then, in the late nineteenth century came the rise of Darwinism, which gradually altered the way much of the world thinks about the origins of the universe and the nature of human life. The consequence of these ideas is that we now live in a society where human autonomy is worshiped and viewing the Bible as the authoritative word of God is seen to be radically superstitious, if not dangerous. Moreover, ethics have changed in the Western world. Cohabitation, divorce, abortion, and homosexuality are all considered to be perfectly normal. To identify any of these things as sinful behavior will immediately earn you the labels of hateful, judgmental, intolerant, and extreme.

Paul says that this seismic shift in thinking will be characteristic of the last days. The world will not increase in righteousness. According to what the apostle says in this passage, we ought not expect a golden age of morality and peace before the return of Christ. Instead, he describes a world filled with the love of self rather than the love of God.

The Trouble That Is to Come

In 3:2–5, Paul catalogs nineteen evil characteristics of the last days. His list begins and ends with an emphasis on misplaced love: "For men will be lovers of themselves, lovers of money...lovers of pleasure rather than lovers of God" (3:2a, 4b). These particular descriptions of societal degeneration serve as bookends on a library of licentiousness that Paul details. They provide the key to the rest of the list. "Moral corruption follows from love falsely directed," notes Donald Guthrie. "Self-centeredness, and material advantages, when they become the chief objects of affection, destroy all moral values, and the subsequent list of vices is their fruit."[3]

Narcissism (the love of self), greed (the love of money), and hedonism (the love of pleasure) were familiar traits in the city of Ephesus. With its thriving economy and pagan spirituality that centered largely on its Temple of Artemis, Ephesus was a sophisticated, cosmopolitan home to lovers of self, money, and pleasure "rather than lovers of God" (3:4). This was the context in which Timothy labored as a minister.

Narcissism, greed, and hedonism are also apt descriptions of modern American society. We have become a people who think too highly of ourselves, so much so that sociologists are calling it an epidemic, especially among younger generations.[4] We are also a nation that worships money and lives to obtain more. And we are a culture incurably obsessed with entertainment, spending billions of dollars every year on amusement despite recessions or downturns in the economy. Although there have been important instances of moral progress in America, such as women's suffrage and the end of the African slave trade, there is enough self-love and social illness that it is not difficult to see a reflection of our society in Paul's words.

The subsequent list of vices begins with three expressions that expand on the meaning of self-love. People who love themselves more than God become proud, arrogant, and abusive (3:2). One modern example of this is the sheer lack of respect people show one another on the internet. Pride, arrogance, and abusive speech have become the accepted norm in tweets and social media posts in every level of society, from the middle school bully to the president

---

3. Guthrie, *Pastoral Epistles*, 174.

4. See, for example, two volumes by Jean Twenge: *Generation Me: Why Today's Young Americans Are More Confident, Assertive, Entitled—and More Miserable Than Ever Before* (New York: Atria Books, 2014); and *The Narcissism Epidemic: Living in the Age of Entitlement* (New York: Atria Books, 2010).

of the United States. Christians should be mindful of their conduct in every area of life, including the internet, that "God resists the proud, but gives grace to the humble" (James 4:6; cf. 1 Peter 5:5; Prov. 3:34, respectively).

The next five words in Paul's list of vices focus largely on family life: "disobedient to parents, unthankful, unholy, unloving, unforgiving" (3:2b–3a). In an ideal society, the relationship of children to their parents should be marked by obedience, respect, gratitude, and affection. But in a society where self is worshiped, this is turned upside down, violating the natural order God created (e.g., Ex. 20:12; Deut. 5:16; 21:18–21; Rom. 1:30; 1 Tim. 1:9). We see this in our culture today more than ever, with parents making the child the center of the family's life, fathers depicted as buffoons in film and television, and divorced moms and dads calling "co-parenting" a viable option to the commitment of marriage. The fruit of these things is a people who are ungrateful, heartless, and unappeasable.

The next seven expressions extend beyond the family: "slanderers, without self-control, brutal, despisers of good, traitors, headstrong, haughty" (3:3b–4a). We see examples of this behavior everywhere today. We have become tragically accustomed to slanderous attacks on our favorite news channel by someone who does not share another's political convictions. We see violent, reckless protests by those frustrated with social injustice. Although we have made great advancements in technology, medicine, and engineering, we seem powerless to truly live with one another in peace and decency.

Paul adds in 3:5 that these times of difficulty are not confined to a pagan society but will also negatively influence the church: "having a form of godliness but denying its power." Paul describes professing Christians who give lip service to the gospel but ultimately look to themselves rather than the gospel for life-changing power. They may practice an external form of religion, but in their actual beliefs they are practical atheists.

Unfortunately, this has become the common theme in modern American evangelicalism. Market research guru George Barna has observed, "To millions of Americans, God—if we even believe in a supernatural deity—exists for the pleasure of humankind. He resides in the heavenly realm solely for our utility and benefit. Although we are too clever to voice it, we live by the notion that true power is accessed not by looking upward but by turning inward."[5] To assume that God exists for us rather than we for God is to reject the true source of godliness, despite any outward appearance of godliness. Barna warns about the consequences of such a spiritual approach: "It will be every man for himself, with no second thoughts or regrets about the personal or societal implications of this incredibly selfish, nihilistic, narcissistic way of life."[6] Barna concludes, "In short, the spirituality of America is Christian in name only.... We desire experience more than knowledge. We prefer choices to absolutes. We embrace preferences rather than truths. We seek comfort rather than growth. Faith must come on our terms or we reject it. We have enthroned ourselves as the final arbiters of righteousness, the ultimate rulers of our own experience and destiny. We are the Pharisees of the new millennium."[7]

Similarly, sociologist Christian Smith has labeled popular culture's Christianity "Moralistic, Therapeutic Deism."[8] His extensive research on teen and young adult spirituality has shown that the dominant form of Christianity in America is less interested in truth than in therapy and more focused on consumers than on discipleship. Smith defines the basic tenets of Moralistic Therapeutic Deism as follows:

1. God created the world.
2. God wants people to be good, nice, and fair to each other, as taught in the Bible and most world religions.

---

5. George Barna, *The Second Coming of the Church* (Nashville: Word, 1998), 7.
6. Barna, *Second Coming of the Church*, 8.
7. Barna, *Second Coming of the Church*, 23.
8. Christian Smith with Melinda Lundquist Denton, *Soul Searching: The Religious and Spiritual Lives of American Teenagers* (New York: Oxford University Press, 2006), 162–71, 258, 262.

3. The central goal of life is to be happy and to feel good about oneself.
4. God does not need to be particularly involved in one's life except when needed to resolve a problem.
5. Good people go to heaven when they die.[9]

Contrary to previous generations that possessed at least some basic knowledge of the Bible and, in many cases, could recite the Apostles' Creed, many professing Christians today seem to have very little ability to articulate the gospel and why they believe it.

Paul tells Timothy that such a gospel-denying, counterfeit Christianity should be avoided and resisted: "And from such people turn away!" (3:5b). Paul was not implying that Timothy should avoid all contact with unbelievers or shun people who need proper instruction in the faith. Ministers, like their Lord, are called to reach out to sinners in love (Matt. 9:11; Luke 15:2; 19:7). As Paul says elsewhere, to have no association with sinners whatsoever would require one to "go out of the world" (1 Cor. 5:10; see vv. 9–13). Instead, Paul means that Timothy was not to tolerate a Christless Christianity or those in the church who promote it.

To this, the apostle adds, "For of this sort are those who creep into households and make captives of gullible women loaded down with sins, led away by various lusts, always learning and never able to come to the knowledge of the truth" (3:6–7). Some forms of counterfeit Christianity are more aggressive than others. We think of the cults that have plagued the world by promoting their false doctrines in the name of Christ, whether the Gnostics in the early church or the Mormons and Jehovah's Witnesses in our modern day. In their methods of proselytizing, they often prey on households, going door to door, sometimes targeting vulnerable women

9. Smith and Denton, *Soul Searching*, as quoted in Michael Horton, *Christless Christianity: The Alternative Gospel of the American Church* (Grand Rapids: Baker Books, 2008), 41.

who are weighed down emotionally. They search for those who make easy converts.

Paul cites an example of these heretical vultures in 3:8: "Now as Jannes and Jambres resisted Moses, so do these also resist the truth: men of corrupt minds, disapproved concerning the faith." According to Jewish tradition, Jannes and Jambres were the magicians in Pharaoh's court who opposed Moses. Their names do not appear in the Old Testament but were preserved through oral tradition and Jewish historical writings. Paul uses them as examples of "imposters" (3:13) who oppose the truth. Just as Jannes and Jambres opposed Moses, so also false teachers had opposed Paul and were now opposing Timothy. And just as Moses proclaimed the word of God and did not waver from the truth, so too must Timothy do the same, even in the face of opposition.

Paul concludes this section by offering Timothy some encouragement: "But they will progress no further, for their folly will be manifest to all, as theirs also was" (3:9). Indeed, the days are evil, as Paul has explained in 3:1–8, but they are also numbered. The times of difficulty will not continue forever. The last days eventually will come to an end when Christ returns to "judge the living and the dead" (4:1).

But what are we to do in the meantime? How is Christianity supposed to survive during such dark days of difficulty? What can possibly change people from being lovers of self to being lovers of God?

The Word in Which We Trust

Paul has painted a dismal picture of the last days in order to help Timothy understand the urgency of preaching the word of God faithfully. He wants Timothy to put his confidence not in himself but in the word, which alone is able to make one "wise for salvation through faith which is in Christ Jesus" (3:15b). This is why Paul goes on in 3:16–17 to speak of the authority of Scripture and in 4:1–5 to charge him to preach the Scriptures. Nothing but the power of the gospel can change the radical corruption of the human heart.

"Only the gospel offers a radical solution to this problem," says John Stott. "For the gospel promises a new birth or new creation, which involves being turned inside out, from self to unself, a real re-orientation of mind and conduct, and which makes us fundamentally God-centered instead of self-centered. Then, when God is first and self is last, we love the world God loves and seek to give and serve like him."[10]

The church today must have confidence in the word of God. We are too easily tempted to look for external solutions to the internal problem of sin. We tend to think that more laws or better public policies can produce righteousness in the human heart, that if we just elect the right leaders or pass the right laws, the times of difficulty will come to an end. Certainly, as Christians, we are called to love our neighbor and be good citizens, doing all we can to "overcome evil with good" (Rom. 12:21). Likewise, the magistrate has the God-given responsibility of suppressing vice in society, promoting justice, and being "an avenger…on him who practices evil" (13:4). But we must always remember that the godlessness in the last days described by Paul in 3:1–9 cannot be overcome by laws and public policies. Not even the Ten Commandments can change the human heart. The persistent rebellion and idolatry of Israel, the nation to whom God had given His law and with whom He made a covenant, shows us the impotency of the law. The law can, to some extent, expose and restrain sin, but it cannot produce righteousness. It is powerless to change the human heart from being a lover of self to being a lover of God. As Paul said in Galatians 3:21, "For if there had been a law given which could have given life, truly righteousness would have been by the law."

Several years ago this point was powerfully illustrated to me when my son came home from the San Diego Zoo and told about what he saw that day at the tiger exhibit. While watching a Malayan tiger through a window in its large, walled-in enclosure, he noticed a wild duck land within the confines of the tiger's domain. The duck

10. Stott, *Message of 2 Timothy*, 82.

appeared totally unaware that it had landed in a tiger's exhibit. For all the duck knew, it had found a lovely and lush part of San Diego, a wonderful place to take a rest. But the tiger's eye caught the duck's landing and was watching its every move. Oblivious to the presence of the tiger, the duck waddled over to the stream to take a drink. The tiger instinctively and quietly assumed an attack position and then bolted for the duck in a flash. Before the duck even saw the tiger coming, it was in the jaws of the powerful creature, which tore it to shreds and consumed it as a meal. Although the tiger lived within the walls of the San Diego Zoo, it could not cease from doing what came naturally. The walls could restrain the tiger, at least to a certain extent, and defined its boundaries of living, but they were powerless to change the tiger's nature. They could not keep the tiger from being a tiger, as the duck discovered on that day.

The law is similar to the walls of the tiger's exhibit. The law defines the boundaries within which we are to live, and to a certain extent it can restrain sin. But it is powerless to change hearts. For that we need the gospel, which the Holy Spirit is pleased to use in all of His re-creative power to renew our minds and reshape our hearts. The gospel announces to us that a new creation has dawned in Jesus Christ and brings us into union with our Savior so that we begin to walk in newness of life and grateful obedience to God. It begins changing our hearts, transforming our love for self into love for God and neighbor. Where there once was pride, arrogance, abusive behavior, ingratitude, unholiness, slander, recklessness, and conceit (e.g., 3:2–4), the Spirit begins to bear the fruit of "love, joy, peace, longsuffering, kindness, goodness, faithfulness, gentleness, [and] self-control. Against such there is no law" (Gal. 5:22–23). Only the gospel can do this, which is why it needs to be preached faithfully and frequently.

Do we have confidence in the preaching of God's word? Do we truly believe that "the word of God is not chained" (2 Tim. 2:9)? Do we trust that God is able to use His word even in the darkest of days and most difficult of times?

One man who demonstrated confidence in the word of God was a Scottish Presbyterian minister by the name of Robert Morrison, one of the very first Protestant missionaries to the Chinese. In 1805 the London Missionary Society recruited Morrison to go to China and put him on a ship to make the long voyage. When the owner of the ship heard about Morrison's plans, he was skeptical. "And so, Mr. Morrison," he said, "do you really expect that you will make any spiritual impact on the idolatry of the great Chinese Empire?"

"No sir," Morrison replied, "but I expect God will."[11] After twenty-five years of labor, he completed a translation of the entire Bible in the Chinese language. He also baptized ten Chinese believers, some of whom became ministers and evangelists.

Herein lies the answer to how Christianity will survive times of difficulty in the last days. It will survive the same way it did in the first century, when it passed from Paul to Timothy, and from Timothy to "faithful men who will be able to teach others also" (2 Tim. 2:2). It will survive in the same way it has since the days of Robert Morrison as he preached the word in a closed and oppressive society like China. It will survive in our own day, even as we see Christianity moving into cultural exile. It will be passed on to the next generation not by Christians winning all the culture wars but by guarding the good deposit of the gospel and making disciples of Jesus Christ. The word of God will endure, even in the last days.

May we be faithful to hear, read, and meditate on the word of God. May we be mindful of the times in which we live, but let us also put our trust in God and His word, for His word will endure forever.

---

11. R. Li-Hua, *Competitiveness of Chinese Firms: West Meets East* (London: Palgrave Macmillan, 2014), 40.

10

Sola Scriptura

2 TIMOTHY 3:10–17

But you have carefully followed my doctrine, manner of life, purpose, faith, longsuffering, love, perseverance, persecutions, afflictions, which happened to me at Antioch, at Iconium, at Lystra—what persecutions I endured. And out of them all the Lord delivered me. Yes, and all who desire to live godly in Christ Jesus will suffer persecution. But evil men and impostors will grow worse and worse, deceiving and being deceived. But you must continue in the things which you have learned and been assured of, knowing from whom you have learned them, and that from childhood you have known the Holy Scriptures, which are able to make you wise for salvation through faith which is in Christ Jesus.

All Scripture is given by inspiration of God, and is profitable for doctrine, for reproof, for correction, for instruction in righteousness, that the man of God may be complete, thoroughly equipped for every good work.

In 1522 an English scholar by the name of William Tyndale was having dinner with a noted Roman Catholic clergyman when the conversation turned to the new theological ideas surfacing on the European continent. These concepts, promoted in large part by Martin Luther, were being debated within the halls of universities and monasteries. Many people were becoming convinced that only Scripture, and not the pope, has the final word on all matters of faith and doctrine. This principle became known as *sola Scriptura* (Scripture alone). It, along with the other four *solas*—*sola gratia* (by grace alone), *sola fide* (through faith alone), *solus Christus* (in Christ alone), and *soli Deo gloria* (to the glory of God alone)—became the battle cry of the Protestant Reformation.

Tyndale, an Oxford- and Cambridge-trained linguist, was among those making that cry. He was determined to translate the Bible into English, believing that it should be made available to the common people in their common tongue rather than only in Latin, as was the case at that time. He was also persuaded that God's Word should be read and preached in the vernacular during public worship, since the way for people to know Christ is through the Word. After hearing Tyndale's convictions, the Catholic scholar became agitated and exclaimed, "We are better to be without God's laws than the Pope's!"

Tyndale replied, "I defy the Pope and all his laws.... If God spare my life ere many years, I will cause a boy that driveth the plow, shall know more of the Scriptures than thou dost."[1]

Four years later, while hiding in Germany, Tyndale finished the first English translation of the Greek New Testament and began smuggling it into his native England, where it was banned. Thousands of copies, including several pirated editions, made their way into the hands of English speakers. Tyndale's labors would eventually cost him his life.

What drove Tyndale to risk so much? Why would a man of his education and training choose to put all of his effort into such a dangerous project? Fluent in Latin, Italian, French, Spanish, and German and competent to handle Greek and Hebrew texts, Tyndale could have spent his days comfortably as a scholar. Why did he instead choose such a hazardous vocation that caused him to live in hiding and die a martyr? It was because Tyndale knew that the Bible is unlike any other book in the world. It is the very word of God and reveals the only solution to humankind's greatest problem. Sinful and helpless to save themselves, humans need a Savior, someone to pay the debt they owe and provide them with the righteousness

1. John Foxe, *Foxe's Book of Martyrs* (New Kensington, Penn.: Whitaker House, 1981), 138–39.

they need. That Savior is Jesus Christ, who is revealed by the Scriptures which are "profitable for doctrine, for reproof, for correction, for instruction in righteousness, that the man of God may be complete, thoroughly equipped for every good work" (2 Tim. 3:16–17).

The apostle Paul makes this declaration about the Scriptures after reminding Timothy of his long familiarity with them and their central purpose of making one "wise for salvation through faith which is in Christ Jesus" (3:15). Having described in 3:1–9 the darkness of the last days, Paul now shines a bright light of encouragement as he makes a positive assessment of his spiritual son and exhorts him to continue in what he has learned: "But you have carefully followed my doctrine, manner of life, purpose, faith, longsuffering, love, perseverance, persecutions, afflictions" (3:10–11a). Unlike the "evil men and imposters" who exemplify the times of difficulty, people "will grow worse and worse, deceiving and being deceived" (3:13).

Timothy had been a dedicated disciple of the apostle, both in doctrine and in life. For several years, he had absorbed Paul's theology and followed his example. He must remain on that path after Paul's death: "But you must continue in the things which you have learned and been assured of," the aged apostle exhorts his young colleague, "knowing from whom you have learned them" (3:14). The one from whom Timothy had learned was Paul, who had trained Timothy for the ministry and prepared him for the future. But his instructors also included people from his childhood—namely, his mother Eunice and his grandmother Lois, women who were known for their godliness and sincere faith (1:5). The word in which Timothy had been trained and raised from his youth must now be preached. As part of his encouragement to his younger colleague to preach the word and suffer for the gospel, Paul pens an important statement about the perfections of Scripture—that it is authoritative, necessary, perspicuous, and sufficient.

Scripture Is Authoritative

In 2 Timothy 3:16, Paul affirms the authority of Scripture by reminding Timothy of its origin: "All Scripture is given by inspiration of

God." The word translated "Scripture" (*graphe*) was "used in the Greek of the day for any piece of writing, but in the NT it is used only of holy scripture."[2] Like the term "Holy Scriptures" (NKJV) or "sacred writings" (ESV) in 3:15, the comprehensive expression "all Scripture" refers to the thirty-nine books of the Old Testament canon along with the emerging new revelation that would eventually become the recognized twenty-seven books of the New Testament. The latter included Paul's own writings, which he directed churches to read publicly and alongside the Old Testament (e.g., Col. 4:16; 1 Thess. 5:27). As an apostle, Paul spoke with the authority of Christ Himself (1 Cor. 2:13; 2 Cor. 2:17). His message was received as the very word of God by both congregations (Gal. 4:14; 1 Thess. 2:13) and other apostles (2 Peter 3:15–16). Paul stresses that *all*, not some or even most, of Scripture is breathed out by God.[3]

The Greek word translated "given by inspiration of God" (*theopneustos*) emphasizes that the Bible is a book written by humans but entirely divine in origin. As the apostle Peter says, Scripture was not produced "by the will of man, but holy men of God spoke as they were moved by the Holy Spirit" (2 Peter 1:21). God breathed out His word in the sense that He organically inspired each author

---

2. Knight, *Pastoral Epistles*, 445.

3. There has been a considerable amount of exegetical debate on verse 16 regarding where to place the verb "is" and how to interpret the Greek word *kai*, which can mean either "and" or "even, also." If the passage in Greek is translated "all Scripture is breathed out by God and profitable," as the ESV states it, "breathed out by God" and "profitable" are taken as two predicate adjectives joined by "and" (*kai*). In this case, the statement affirms that the whole biblical canon is divine in origin, authoritative, and profitable. But if the word "is" is placed after "breathed out by God" and the Greek word *kai* is translated not as "and" but "also," it leaves open the possibility that not all of Scripture is inspired by God. Both translations are grammatically possible. Several scholars have argued convincingly for the former translation and shown that what Paul says here to Timothy embodies a theological conviction found throughout the New Testament and held by Christ, the apostles, and other New Testament writers. See Knight, *Pastoral Epistles*, 444–50; Towner, *Letters to Timothy and Titus*, 585–94; Mounce, *Pastoral Epistles*, 565–70; Liefeld, *NIV Application Commentary: 1 & 2 Timothy, Titus*, 279–81; Guthrie, *Pastoral Epistles*, 181–83.

of Scripture to bring His revelation into the world. Rather than mechanically dictating His word and bypassing the human agent altogether, the Holy Spirit used the particular language, diction, personality, and style of each individual writer, "breathing out" His word through the writer and bringing it into existence.[4] Scripture is God's speech—His word—and His word is authoritative.

This was a crucial reminder for Timothy as he faced false teachers and competing truth claims in Ephesus. He needed reassurance about and confidence in the Bible he believed and preached. Paul sought to fortify his confidence in Scripture by reminding him that it is authoritative and "profitable for doctrine, for reproof, for correction, for instruction in righteousness" (2 Tim. 3:16b). Timothy was armed with the most formidable weapon to "wage the good warfare" (1 Tim. 1:18) against false teaching.

Christians today need that same confidence. The world is full of competing truth claims. It has been this way ever since the serpent twisted God's words and offered to Eve an alternative route to the good life: "Has God indeed said, 'You shall not eat of every tree of the garden'?.... You will not surely die" (Gen. 3:1, 4). From the beginning, it has been the devil's modus operandi to cause people to doubt and disbelieve God's word. His methods are crafty and deceitful. He disguises himself as "an angel of light" (2 Cor. 11:14), using the popular truth claims in the world to cast suspicion on the authority of Scripture. Whether it is Oprah Winfrey's "wisdom" for living, Richard Dawkins's bold assertions about evolution, or Joel Osteen's promise that you can have your best life right now, the world has no shortage of popular pundits and gurus who make truth claims that compete with God's revelation. How are we to sift through these claims? How should we think about God, morality, relationships, suffering, death, and the meaning of life? Is there a

4. For more on the use of *theopneustos* and the divine inspiration of Scripture, see B. B. Warfield, *The Inspiration and Authority of the Bible* (Philadelphia: Presbyterian and Reformed, 1948), 245–96.

universal standard to which we can appeal? Or is each person the final authority in determining what is true and what is false?

To these important questions the apostle Paul says that "all Scripture is given by inspiration of God, and is profitable for doctrine, for reproof, for correction, for instruction in righteousness" (2 Tim. 3:16). The Bible is the final standard of truth, for there can be no higher authority than God Himself. We are compelled, therefore, to submit to Scripture.

Scripture Is Necessary

Paul points out that Scripture is necessary to make "the man of God…complete, thoroughly equipped for every good work" (2 Tim. 3:17). The phrase "the man of God" is a description that can apply to church leaders like Timothy (see 1 Tim. 6:11). Taken in this sense, the expression describes how, as Donald Guthrie noted, "the Christian minister has in his hands a God-given instrument designed to equip him completely for his work."[5] But the phrase can also apply to any Christian in general. The Holy Spirit uses the means of Scripture to sanctify the child of God and bring him or her to completion in Christ. Jesus prayed, "Holy Father…sanctify them by Your truth. Your word is truth" (John 17:11, 17). Apart from Scripture, we cannot grow in our sanctification. Recognizing the necessity of Scripture for our spiritual growth, the early church father John Chrysostom affirmed, "For thence we shall know, whether we ought to learn or to be ignorant of anything. And thence we may disprove what is false, thence we may be corrected and brought to a right mind, may be comforted and consoled, and if anything is deficient, we may have it added to us."[6]

Scripture is necessary, though, for believers not only to grow in their sanctification and knowledge of Christ but also to be brought to faith in Christ in the first place. As Paul said to the Romans,

5. Guthrie, *Pastoral Epistles*, 182.

6. Chrysostom, *The Commentary and Homilies of St. John Chrysostom*, in *Nicene and Post-Nicene Fathers*, vol. 13 (Peabody, Mass.: Hendrickson, 2012), 510.

"How then shall they call on Him in whom they have not believed? And how shall they believe in Him of whom they have not heard? And how shall they hear without a preacher? And how shall they preach unless they are sent?… So then faith comes by hearing, and hearing by the word of God" (Rom. 10:14–15a, 17). The gospel cannot be discovered by the light of nature. We cannot hear the gospel in the wind or see it written in the stars. Nor can we learn of it from our own experience apart from the Scriptures. The gospel is an external message about the life, death, and resurrection of Jesus Christ that must be proclaimed to us so that we can put our trust in Christ and be saved.

It is for this reason that Reformed theology has made the classic distinction between general revelation and special revelation. As the Belgic Confession, article 2 states,

> We know God by two means: First, by the creation, preservation, and government of the universe; which is before our eyes as a most beautiful book, wherein all creatures, great and small, are as so many letters leading us to perceive clearly the invisible things of God, namely, His eternal power and deity, as the apostle Paul says (Rom 1:20). All these things are sufficient to convict men and leave them without excuse. Second, He makes Himself more clearly and fully known to us by His holy and divine Word as far as is necessary for us in this life, to His glory and our salvation.

General revelation declares the glory of God, but it cannot preach the grace of God in Christ. It is not designed to tell sinners how they can be right with God through the righteousness of Christ. Humankind needs God's special revelation, His breathed-out Scriptures, in order to obtain knowledge of the gospel and the plan of redemption.

Scripture Is Perspicuous

Scripture is not only authoritative and necessary but also perspicuous—that is to say, clear in its message. "All Scripture is…

profitable for doctrine," Paul says in 2 Timothy 3:16. Although some parts of Scripture are clearer than others, there is no part that is so obscure that it is unprofitable. All of it is "profitable for doctrine, for reproof, for correction, for instruction in righteousness." More importantly, the basic message of Scripture is crystal clear—namely, that God is holy, man is a sinner, but God has sent Christ to do for man what he could not do for himself. As the apostle says in 3:15, "The Holy Scriptures...are able to make you wise for salvation through faith which is in Christ Jesus."

The medieval church claimed that the Bible is too murky and mysterious to understand without the guidance of the pope and church tradition. In the sixteenth century, as part of the Roman Catholic Church's Counter-Reformation, the Council of Trent argued that Scripture and church tradition are two equal forms of God's word. This word consists not only of "the written books" of the biblical canon but also of "the unwritten traditions" that the pope has the privilege of determining. Both Scripture and the unwritten traditions are, in the Roman Catholic Church, "received and venerated with an equal affection of piety and reverence," as both have been "preserved in the Catholic Church by a continuous succession."[7]

Against this, the Protestant Reformers argued that Scripture alone is the God-breathed, final authority for all matters on faith and it is clear in its presentation of the gospel. The fact that not all parts of the Bible are equally clear does not demand that the unwritten traditions of the church be raised to the same place of authority as the Scriptures. The Westminster Confession of Faith 1.7 explains the perspicuity of Scripture as follows: "All things in Scripture are not alike plain in themselves nor alike clear unto all. Yet, those things that are necessary to be known, believed, and observed for salvation are so clearly propounded, and opened in some place of Scripture or another, that not only the learned, but the unlearned, in a due use of the ordinary means, may attain unto

---

7. *The Canons and Decrees of the Sacred and Ecumenical Council of Trent*, trans. J. Waterworth (London, 1848), 18.

a sufficient understanding of them." In other words, not everything in Scripture is easy to understand, but all that we must understand in order to be saved is clear.

It is always important to remember that the Bible is ultimately about one thing: God redeeming a people for Himself through Jesus Christ. From Genesis to Revelation, that is Scripture's one message. We must remember the clarity of that message when coming to the Bible. We must not lose the forest for the sake of the trees. As Edmund Clowney warned, "It is possible to know Bible stories, yet miss *the* Bible story":

> The Bible is much more than William How stated: "a golden casket where gems of truth are stored." It is more than a bewildering collection of oracles, proverbs, poems, architectural directions, annals, and prophecies. The Bible has a story line. It traces an unfolding drama. The story follows the history of Israel, but it does not begin there, nor does it contain what you would expect in a national history. The narrative does not pay tribute to Israel. Rather, it regularly condemns Israel and justifies God's severest judgments. The story is God's story. It describes His work to rescue rebels from their folly, guilt, and ruin.[8]

In other words, the Bible is about Jesus and what He has accomplished. The perspicuity of Scripture is why Jesus said, "The Scriptures…testify of Me" (John 5:39). They explain clearly how Christ has "abolished death and brought life and immortality to light through the gospel" (2 Tim. 1:10).

Scripture Is Sufficient

Paul specifies how Scripture is "profitable for doctrine" by adding that it is for "instruction in righteousness, that the man of God may be complete, thoroughly equipped for every good work" (2 Tim. 3:16–17). The Bible does not tell us everything we need to

---

8. Edmund Clowney, *The Unfolding Mystery: Discovering Christ in the Old Testament* (Phillipsburg, N.J.: P&R, 1988), 11.

know for life as human beings. It does not teach us algebra, chemistry, or Italian. Nevertheless, that which it does teach is enough for us to know God and be complete in Christ. As John Stott said, "The Bible is essentially a handbook of salvation." He explained:

> Its over-arching purpose is to teach not facts of science which men can discover by their own empirical investigation, but facts of salvation, which no space exploration can discover but only God can reveal. The whole Bible unfolds the divine scheme of salvation—man's creation in God's image, his fall through disobedience into sin and under judgment, God's continuing love for him in spite of his rebellion, God's eternal plan to save him through his covenant of grace with a chosen people, culminating in Christ; the coming of Christ as the Saviour, who died to bear man's sin, was raised from death, was exalted to heaven and sent the Holy Spirit; and man's rescue first from guilt and alienation, then from bondage, and finally from mortality in his progressive experience of the liberty of God's children. None of this would be known apart from the biblical revelation.[9]

The biblical revelation must be interpreted and explained if we are to understand what we are to believe and how we are to live, but its sufficiency means that we need no other source of special revelation in addition to Scripture.

This should be a tremendous encouragement to all Christian parents to remain faithful in their callings and disciple the children whom God has entrusted to them. Bring them to Jesus through the word of God, which is sufficient "to make [them] wise for salvation" (2 Tim. 3:15)! We cannot control outcomes, but we can control what we choose to do with the time that is given to us. Timothy's grandmother Lois and his mother, Eunice, chose to make it a priority to familiarize Timothy with the Bible, which, at the time of Timothy's childhood, was the Old Testament Scriptures. Timothy cut his teeth on the word of God, which has sufficient power to convert us, sanctify us, and make us wise for salvation through faith in Christ Jesus.

---

9. Stott, *Message of 2 Timothy*, 102.

Parents: be confident in the sufficiency of the word of God. Read the Bible to and with your children. Pray for and with them. Bring them to worship with God's people, where they will hear Christ preached consistently. Be patient with them, even when they seem disinterested or express their doubts about the word of God. Continue to love them as they grow, patiently helping them to know what we believe and why we believe it. The family is a discipleship group even if, as in Timothy's case, one parent does not believe (Acts 16:1–3). The church is in need of more women like Lois and Eunice, confident in the sufficiency of Scripture.

The sufficiency of Scripture, like its authority, necessity, and perspicuity, means that the Bible is truly of infinite and perennial value to human beings. It alone is the God-breathed revelation that shows us the grace and glory of Christ. It was for this reason that William Tyndale was willing to suffer and sacrifice so much.

In 1536 Tyndale was tried for heresy, convicted, and condemned to death. On the day of his execution, at forty-two years of age, he was tied to a stake to be burned as a heretic. As the flames began to rise, Tyndale cried out his final words: "Lord! open the King of England's eyes."[10] The king who had long suppressed the Bible in Tyndale's homeland became the object of this martyr's last protest. But Tyndale's death was not in vain. Within four years, four English translations of the Bible, each based on Tyndale's work, were published in England. Indeed, we have English Bibles today largely because of Tyndale's labors and sacrifice.

Let us cherish the Scriptures not only because they have come to us in our own language through the blood of martyrs but especially because they are the authoritative word of God, necessary for our knowledge of Christ, clear in their presentation of the gospel, and sufficient to equip us for every good work.

---

10. Foxe, *Book of Martyrs*, 152.

11

Preach the Word!

2 TIMOTHY 4:1–5

I charge you therefore before God and the Lord Jesus Christ, who will judge the living and the dead at His appearing and His kingdom: Preach the word! Be ready in season and out of season. Convince, rebuke, exhort, with all longsuffering and teaching. For the time will come when they will not endure sound doctrine, but according to their own desires, because they have itching ears, they will heap up for themselves teachers; and they will turn their ears away from the truth, and be turned aside to fables. But you be watchful in all things, endure afflictions, do the work of an evangelist, fulfill your ministry.

So far in 2 Timothy Paul has urged Timothy to use his spiritual gifts for ministry (1:6–7), suffer with him for the gospel (1:8, 11–12; 2:3, 9–10; 3:12), guard the truth (1:13–14), instruct faithful men who can teach others (2:2), and remain self-disciplined (2:3–5, 15, 20–26; 3:10–14). Chapter 4, however, brings us to the apostle's focal point of the epistle: "I charge you therefore before God and the Lord Jesus Christ, who will judge the living and the dead at His appearing and His kingdom: Preach the word!" (4:1–2). As a pastor, Timothy must preach the word with authority, urgency, and fidelity.

We Need to Hear the Word Preached with Authority

Immediately after emphasizing that Scripture is authoritative and the final standard of truth (3:16–17), Paul solemnly charges Timothy to proclaim that same truth. Armed with God's authorized weapon against false teaching and competing truth claims, Timothy was to "wage the good warfare" (1 Tim. 1:18) by preaching the word boldly and confidently, recognizing that the message he carried was not his own, but God's. The verb Paul uses for "charge" in 4:1 (*diamartyromai*) has legal connotations, evoking the idea of testifying under oath in a court of law. In other words, Paul is not merely *suggesting* that Timothy preach the word but giving him an official commission to go forth as an appointed ambassador for Christ's kingdom, proclaiming the word of the King in all of its authority.

A preacher's popularity, speaking skills, or "pulpit presence" do not give him authority. Nor does his authority derive from his academic degrees, ministerial credentials, or position in the church. The authority he possesses comes only from the Bible, which he has been called and ordained to preach. Apart from the authoritative word of God, he has no authority of his own. His authority is not *magisterial*—that is, inherent in his position—but *ministerial*, inherent in the word that he is called to serve to others. Jesus did not tell Peter to rule over his sheep, but to tend and feed them (John 21:16–17). When the pastor steps into the pulpit before the people of God, he stands there not confident in himself or his credentials, but rather in the divine meal he has been sent to serve, the authoritative word that he has been sent to proclaim.

The world needs to hear the word of God boldly proclaimed by men who believe in its authority. The church needs ministers who are unashamed of the gospel and committed to the essential doctrines of the Christian faith. In the past century, there has been a steady deterioration of authoritative preaching. More than fifty years ago, the noted Welsh preacher D. Martyn Lloyd-Jones spoke about this erosion in a series of lectures he delivered at Westminster Theological Seminary in Philadelphia on the subject of preaching and preachers. In his first address, he outlined several reasons why, during the twentieth century, the church had seen a decline of good preaching. The first, he said, was "the loss of belief in the authority of the Scriptures":

> If you have not got authority, you cannot speak well, you cannot preach.... While men believed in the Scriptures as the

> authoritative Word of God and spoke on the basis of that authority you had great preaching. But once that went, and men began to speculate, and to theorize, and to put up hypotheses and so on, the eloquence and the greatness of the spoken word inevitably declined and began to wane. You cannot deal with speculations and conjectures in the same way as preaching had formerly dealt with the great themes of the Scriptures. But as belief in the great doctrines of the Bible began to go out, and sermons were replaced by ethical addresses and homilies, and moral uplift and socio-political talk, it is not surprising that preaching declined.[1]

Sadly, things have not improved since Lloyd-Jones made that assessment in the spring of 1969. Nowadays, in churches across America, what often passes for a sermon is not a faithful exposition of the authoritative word of God that boldly proclaims Christ, but a life coach session, political rant, or commentary of the pastor's personal thoughts on how Christians should behave in particular situations. We must realize that these things have no authority in Christ's church. Paul did not commission Timothy to stand in front of God's people and share his personal and unauthoritative opinions. On the contrary, he charged him to preach the word of God with authority!

This is why sermons that proclaim Christ as Redeemer are so important. As Kevin Vanhoozer has noted, "The sermon is the best frontal assault on imaginations held captive by secular stories that promise other ways to the good life."[2] Curved in on ourselves in selfish introspection and idol worship, we need an external word from God, a voice that comes from outside of us to intrude on the make-believe worlds we have foolishly constructed, so that we will hear the truth. The "lively preaching of his Word," as the Heidelberg Catechism 98 puts it, is God's ordained means to accomplish

---

1. D. Martyn Lloyd-Jones, *Preaching and Preachers* (Grand Rapids: Zondervan, 1971), 13.

2. Kevin J. Vanhoozer, *The Drama of Doctrine: A Canonical-Linguistic Approach to Christian Theology* (Louisville, Ky.: Westminster, 2005), 456.

this purpose. God sends His appointed emissary to His covenant people in order to proclaim His covenantal speech from His canon of Scripture. It is an intrusive act, driving us out of ourselves and directing our faith to the promises of God, which in Christ are "Yes" and "Amen" (2 Cor. 1:20). The Westminster Larger Catechism 155 gets at this precise point when it describes how the Holy Spirit makes the word effectual to salvation: "The Spirit of God maketh the reading, but especially the preaching of the word, an effectual means of enlightening, convincing, and humbling sinners; *of driving them out of themselves, and drawing them unto Christ*; of conforming them to his image, and subduing them to his will; of strengthening them against temptations and corruptions; of building them up in grace, and establishing their hearts in holiness and comfort through faith unto salvation" (emphasis added).

But without Christ's divine emissary sent to us, how will we hear? Without an ordained servant to serve us a meal, how will we eat? If faith comes by hearing, and hearing through the word of Christ (Rom. 10:17), then self-feeding will not work. The gospel is counterintuitive to us, as we are hardwired for law by nature. Someone must tell us this good news. Someone must serve us this meal that informs us of what we do not know by nature; namely, that in Christ we have passed from death to life and from judgment to mercy. Without coming to the feast God provides for us, we will inevitably gravitate toward the drive-through lane of therapy and the garbage can of moralism. Preaching is God's merciful act whereby He pulls us away from our toxic self-feast and serves us with His meal of life.

We Need to Hear the Word Preached with Urgency

Paul's exhortation in 2 Timothy 4:2 to "preach the word" is in the aorist tense, which, when taken with the subsequent imperatives in verses 2–5, emphasizes the decisiveness and urgency of the apostle's tone. In other words, Timothy must feel obligated and compelled to preach the word as never before, like a dying man to dying men, for there is nothing more urgent in all the world than the saving of and caring for souls through the public proclamation of Christ's gospel.

For this reason, Paul tells Timothy to "be ready in season and out of season" (4:2). In other words, the pastor must be on hand to preach the word frequently and consistently, not just when it is convenient for him or when he feels up to the task. Christ's sheep must be fed, and the word is their food. As the seventeenth-century English theologian John Owen said, "This feeding is by the preaching of the gospel. He is no pastor who doth not feed his flock. It belongs essentially to the office."[3]

Preaching the word is the minister's primary work. He is called a minister *of the word* because his chief responsibility is to proclaim (*keruxon*) the word of God. Counseling, visitation, writing, and ecclesiastical meetings all have an important place in the pastoral ministry, but none are as vital as proclaiming God's word to God's people week in and week out. Everything else in the pastoral ministry ultimately flows out of this. If the minister is not a preacher, then he is not a pastor. Although it is possible for a man to be eloquent in the pulpit yet lacking love for the congregation (for pastors are sinners like everyone else), it is misleading to say that a minister can be a good preacher but a bad pastor. Preaching and pastoral care are inseparably united. If a minister does not consistently proclaim the gospel, then he cannot be a good pastor. Conversely, if he faithfully preaches Christ every week, then, despite his shortcomings and deficiencies, he is at least doing that which is most important in the pastoral ministry: serving the sheep with the word of God. The pastor must have a sense of urgency to feed Christ's flock.

It is for this reason that Paul exhorts his young colleague: "convince, rebuke, exhort, with all longsuffering and teaching" (4:2b). Convincing and rebuking are never a license for the minister to scold Christ's sheep or bully them, which is why the apostle quickly adds that his preaching must be done patiently and with edification.

---

3. John Owen, Sermon 5, in *The Works of John Owen*, ed. William H. Goold (Edinburgh: Banner of Truth, 1998), 9:453.

Rather, "convince, rebuke, exhort" is an appeal to the pastor to be urgent in his ministry with, as John Stott wisely pointed out, a threefold approach: intellectual, moral, and emotional. "For some people are tormented by doubts and need to be convinced by arguments. Others have fallen into sin and need to be rebuked. Others again are haunted by fears and need to be encouraged. God's Word does all this and more."[4] The pastor must proclaim and apply the word urgently but always "with all longsuffering and teaching."

Urgency is necessary because "the time will come when they will not endure sound doctrine, but according to their own desires, because they have itching ears, they will heap up for themselves teachers; and they will turn their ears away from the truth, and be turned aside to fables" (4:3–4). Indeed, we live in such times! In today's ecclesiastical landscape, it is not difficult to find a church to suit one's own passions. What are you passionate about? Conservative politics? Social justice? Cultural transformation? Christian psychology? Self-help therapy? Positive thinking? There are churches that specialize in each of these topics and many more. But none of these things are the gospel. When they become the message preached, they represent a deviation and subtle alternative to the authentic cuisine that our Lord wants served to His people.

Through the ministry of *His word* (and not ours!), Christ calls His people to come into His restaurant and dine with Him. He stands on the sidewalk, as it were, crying out to passersby, "I have something good prepared for you! Come and eat! Come to My table!" Money is not an issue. In this restaurant, people who cannot pay are welcome. In fact, our money is no good with God. You need only to be hungry to have a reservation:

Ho! Everyone who thirsts,
Come to the waters;
And you who have no money,
Come, buy and eat.
Yes, come, buy wine and milk
Without money and without price. (Isa. 55:1)

---

4. Stott, *Message of 2 Timothy*, 108.

There is no currency we can offer God to receive the redemptive benefits of His meals. We cannot, through our obedience or techniques for self-improvement, buy what He freely gives as a gift. He has already paid the cost in full through His life, death, and resurrection. We now owe nothing. There is no bill. God simply says, "Come and eat!"

The primary purpose of going to church, therefore, is not to serve God but to be served by Him. The same Lord who once rose from supper, laid aside His outer garments, tied a towel around His waist, and washed the feet of His disciples continues to condescend to His followers and serve them in word and sacrament. He summons us to a festive event in the call to worship. Each week, through the ministry of the word, He spreads a table in the wilderness, setting before us excellent food and drink for the soul.

Pastors: you are the servants whom the Lord has called to prepare and serve this food to His beloved people. Be urgent in this task! Be ready in season and out of season! And be faithful.

We Need to Hear the Word Preached with Fidelity

The final part of Paul's charge to Timothy is found in 4:5: "But you be watchful in all things, endure afflictions, do the work of an evangelist, fulfill your ministry." To preach the word faithfully, the Christian minister must heed these three exhortations. To be sober-minded (*nepho*) means to be "well-balanced, self-controlled."[5] In the context of his charge to Timothy, Paul uses this verb to emphasize the need for the Christian minister to cultivate self-control and self-awareness not merely in general but especially in his preaching of the word. The pulpit is no place for a man who is not sober-minded. Aiming to entertain the congregation through excessive humor, lacing sermons with a political agenda, ranting about one's personal scruples, or making illegitimate applications from the text is not faithful preaching. It demonstrates a lack of sober-mindedness.

---

5. Walter Bauer, *A Greek-English Lexicon of the New Testament and Other Early Christian Literature*, ed. and rev. Frederick William Danker, 3rd ed. (Chicago: University of Chicago Press, 2000), 672.

Timothy must also "endure afflictions" as he seeks to be a faithful preacher of the word (cf. 1:8, 12; 2:3, 9). There are many teachings in Scripture that, if preached faithfully, can invite hostility. For example, the biblical doctrines of hell and predestination as well as the Bible's clear teaching on gender and sexuality can be disturbing not only to unbelievers but also to Christ's sheep, especially those who are younger in the faith. As these doctrines arise in the text, the minister must handle them with wisdom, pastoral care, and gentleness. But he must also resist the temptation to avoid them. "Whenever the biblical faith becomes unpopular," said John Stott, "ministers are sorely tempted to mute those elements which give most offense."[6] Pastors must be willing to endure suffering for preaching the truth, which must always be presented with kindness, patience, and the utmost love for the saints (cf. 2:24–25; 4:2).

Above all, faithful preaching will consistently proclaim the person and work of Christ as sufficient for our redemption. This is the meaning of Paul's exhortation to Timothy: "Do the work of an evangelist" (4:5). Although there is a place for personal evangelism in the life and ministry of the pastor, the emphasis here in Paul's charge to Timothy is in connection to preaching the word. For the apostle, preaching the word means preaching Christ (Rom. 1:16–17; 16:25; 1 Cor. 1:23; 2:1–2; 9:16–18; 2 Cor. 4:1, 5–7). In other words, as Thomas Murphy put it, "The one great theme which the preacher must ever bring out from the Word of God and present in the diversified forms it receives from all scriptural truth is Christ and him crucified.... Whatever text or theme, then, is taken by the preacher, it ought to look to Christ. It should be the great burden of every sermon."[7] A sermon that does not center on and clearly present this great theme cannot be called a gospel sermon. It is the proclamation of the gospel—not the skills, personality, charisma, or even personal godliness of the minister—that creates faith in the heart and builds up Christ's church.

---

6. Stott, *Message of 2 Timothy*, 112.
7. Murphy, *Pastoral Theology*, 88.

For this reason, a minister should take heed to the time-tested method of preaching *lectio continua* through whole books of the Bible, for it allows him to proclaim "the whole counsel of God" (Acts 20:27) and provides him with the opportunity to show how the gospel is central in all the Scriptures. The minister of the word must avoid the temptation to skip over significant sections of Old Testament books, such as the genealogies in Genesis, the ceremonial laws in the latter part of Exodus, or the apocalyptic visions in the second half of Daniel, in order to emphasize the more "practical" parts of the book. Such picking and choosing can be irresponsible. We should not try to be wiser than God. He knows what we need far better than we do, and to that end He has given us the whole counsel of His word—genealogies, ceremonial laws, and apocalyptic visions included. The truth is that these sections of Scripture mystify most Christians. It is the preacher's job to explain these passages and show how they are a necessary part of God's redemptive-historical record that climaxes in the person and work of Christ.

To preach Christ from the whole Bible assumes that the Scriptures are not a collection of timeless principles in abstract but rather one coherent record of progressive revelation that tells the story of God redeeming a people for Himself through Jesus Christ. It takes seriously Christ's admonition to the Pharisees, who missed the point of the Old Testament's message: "You search the Scriptures, for in them you think you have eternal life; and these are they which testify of Me" (John 5:39). It is the kind of preaching that Christ Himself delivered to His disciples on the road to Emmaus, where, "beginning at Moses and all the Prophets, He expounded to them in all the Scriptures the things concerning Himself" (Luke 24:27). It applies biblical theology, which, as Graeme Goldsworthy quips, "is nothing more or less than allowing the Bible to speak as a whole: as the one word of the one God about the one way of salvation."[8]

---

8. Graeme Goldsworthy, *Preaching the Whole Bible as Christian Scripture* (Grand Rapids: Eerdmans, 2000), 7.

The minister doing the work of an evangelist also implies that he must make the biblical distinction between the law and the gospel. "The law must be proclaimed in all of its force as God's unmasking of the 'spin' with which we have told the story of our lives," observes Michael Horton, "and the gospel must be proclaimed in all of its joy, as God's own act of clothing us in Christ's righteousness."[9] Preaching that conflates the law and the gospel will inevitably encourage endless introspection rather than pointing people to the sufficiency of Jesus. Invariably, such preaching produces one of two detrimental responses in its hearers: *self-righteousness* or *despair*. As T. David Gordon notes,

> The hearer falls into one of two categories.... One category of listener assumes that the minister is talking about someone *else*, and he rejoices (as did the Pharisee over the tax collector) to hear "the other guy" getting straightened out. Another category of listener eventually capitulates and says: "Okay, I'm not a believer; have it your way. I'm just a horrible, terrible person who's going to hell." But since the sermon mentions Christ only in passing (if at all), the sermon says nothing about the adequacy of Christ as Redeemer, and therefore does nothing to nourish or build faith in him. So true unbelievers are given nothing that might make believers of them, and many true believers are persuaded that they are not believers, and the consolations of Christian faith are taken from them.... No one profits from this kind of preaching; indeed both categories of hearer are harmed by it.[10]

Instead, ministers must be diligent to "do the work of an evangelist" and faithfully preach the law and the gospel. If the preacher does not faithfully proclaim the gospel to the congregation, he will unwittingly serve them food with empty calories. Concerned

9. Michael Horton, *People and Place: A Covenant Ecclesiology* (Louisville, Ky.: Westminister, 2008), 50.

10. T. David Gordon, *Why Johnny Can't Preach: The Media Have Shaped the Messengers* (Phillipsburg, N.J.: P&R, 2009), 83–84.

about consistency in this regard, Iain Murray offers an appropriate admonition to preachers: "It is true that the consequences of faithful preaching are with God and not with us, but are we sure that we are making salvation by Christ's righteousness as clear and prominent as it ought to be? Here is the only message truly relevant to the reality of the condition of fallen men and women. Every offer of hope to individuals which is based upon moral education, self-improvement, or religious devotion, is an empty hope."[11]

Pastors: preach Christ consistently! At the end of the day, this is really all that you have to offer. Preach the word. Be ready in season and out of season. Give them Jesus. Fulfill your ministry.

---

11. Iain Murray, *The Old Evangelicalism* (Edinburgh: Banner of Truth, 2005), 95.

12

Finishing Well

2 TIMOTHY 4:6–8

For I am already being poured out as a drink offering, and the time of my departure is at hand. I have fought the good fight, I have finished the race, I have kept the faith. Finally, there is laid up for me the crown of righteousness, which the Lord, the righteous Judge, will give to me on that Day, and not to me only but also to all who have loved His appearing.

Deep in the crypt of Basilica Sant'Ambrogio, one of the most ancient churches in northern Italy, lies the body of a man who served Christ's church faithfully during the fourth century. Ambrose of Milan (340–397) was a preacher of the word, hymn writer, church planter, defender of orthodoxy, mentor to Augustine, and one of the four "doctors" of the early church. His body is visible to the public eye, resting between two Christian martyrs from the second century: Gervasius on one side, and Protasius on the other. Whatever we may think of the display, Ambrose's legacy as a servant of Christ's church stands as a testimony to one who, by God's grace, fought the good fight, finished the race, and kept the faith. By no means was he perfect, but, like the apostle Paul some three hundred years earlier, he ran hard and finished well. His body awaits the resurrection, which the Lord Jesus has promised to all who trust in Him.

Crossing the finish line should be the goal of every minister of the word. Most pastors are not called to be giants like Ambrose, but all are called to press on and persevere to the end. Sadly, however, many ministers never make it. While the statistics of pastors who burn out and leave the ministry vary from one study to another, all of the data reveals an alarming number of ordained men who battle loneliness, discouragement, and depression. A majority feel that they cannot meet their church's unrealistic expectations, and many frequently doubt their calling. In recent years, there has also been a troubling spike in suicides among pastors. Added to this are the numerous casualties in the ministry due to moral failure and false doctrine. In light of such disconcerting statistics, how can discouraged ministers be encouraged to finish well?

It is not just pastors who can be tempted to quit running the race. Every Christian can experience certain pressures in life that may tempt him or her to lose heart and abandon the church. For example, we think of the college student who is suddenly faced with seemingly irrefutable truth claims against Christianity, the struggling believer who feels hopeless because she is losing her personal battle against sexual immorality, or disillusioned members of a congregation who have experienced the ugliness and shame of a church split. Where can such troubled souls find the courage and motivation to fight the good fight and keep the faith?

The apostle Paul knew the answer. Finding the determination to persevere to the end comes only "in the grace that is in Christ Jesus" (2 Tim. 2:1), His grace that is sufficient even in the midst of our most painful trials, tormenting doubts, and moments of weakness. It was only by the grace of Christ that Paul found the strength to continue during his thirty years of apostolic ministry and finally say at the end of his life, "I have fought the good fight, I have finished the race, I have kept the faith" (4:7). He did not write these words in a time of comfort and ease. He wrote them while incarcerated in Rome and facing the death penalty. He was lonely, cold, and without the necessary tools to redeem the time. Still, he was full of hope, for he knew that the crown of righteousness was laid up for him (4:8) and that the Lord would preserve him "for His heavenly kingdom" (4:18). Convinced that the time of his departure was at hand, Paul penned these verses so that Timothy, a man timid by nature and terrified by opposition, would not be ashamed of his mentor's imprisonment nor despair of his approaching death but see a testimony of the sustaining grace of God, which is sufficient to strengthen every believer to finish well.

An Imminent Death

Paul says in 4:6, "For I am already being poured out as a drink offering, and the time of my departure is at hand." He describes his looming death with a metaphor taken from the Old Testament. Drink offerings were part of the Levitical sacrificial system. In Numbers 15, the Lord commanded that when worshipers brought a lamb to be offered as a burnt offering, they were to bring some wine (approximately one liter) to be poured out with the lamb as an offering to God (vv. 5, 7, 10). Paul draws upon this imagery to describe how his own life was near the end. As wine would be poured out on an altar as a sacrifice to the Lord, so Paul's life was being drained for the sake of Christ and His church. He used the same language in his letter to the Philippians during his first imprisonment in Rome, a time when he was not sure if he would live or die. "Yes, and if I am being poured out as a drink offering on the sacrifice and service of your faith, I am glad and rejoice with you all" (Phil. 2:17). This time, though, he knew his death would be soon. He uses a specific word in Greek to emphasize that his life was *already* being poured out. He is not speculating about his death. Rather, he is certain that this is the end, hence the urgency of his letter to Timothy.

Paul says these things to his beloved son in the faith not to sadden his heart but to encourage him in the work that lay ahead. In one sense, the veteran apostle is telling his young colleague, "Look, I am about to cross the finish line. My race is run. But you, Timothy, you keep running. Preach the word, be sober-minded, do the work of an evangelist, and fulfill your ministry! Don't look back, and don't quit. We'll meet up on the other side of the finish line." Paul was prepared to die. It is not that he was *eager* to die, but that he was *prepared* to die. This was a man who was truly ready to meet his Maker, for he knew that God had justified him on account of the perfect righteousness of Jesus Christ. He was not going to his death in fear or with his head hung low. Instead, he was full of hope because of "the promise of life which is in Christ Jesus" (1:1), the One "who has abolished death and brought life and immortality to light through the gospel" (1:10). Christ abolished death through His resurrection, securing for us glorified life and immortality in the new heaven and new earth.

Meditating on the gospel and our hope of the resurrection is one of the best antidotes to discouragement, both in the Christian ministry and in the Christian life. What could be more encouraging to Timothy than to know that the Christ he served had already abolished death? What could be more encouraging to us when we are tempted to despair? Our Champion has conquered Satan and secured for us the tree of life. Although Christians must still face death, they do so with the assurance that they are already made acceptable to God because they are clothed in Christ's righteousness. Moreover, they will be raised from the dead on the last day to enjoy glorified, eternal life. For Christians, then, death has lost its sting and is no longer to be feared. Because of this glorious good news, we can press on and be "steadfast, immovable, always abounding in the work of the Lord, knowing that your labor is not in vain in the Lord" (1 Cor. 15:58). Being prepared for death is essential to finishing well. The key to preparing for death is to look to Christ, and not ourselves. True faith is not introspective, but extrospective, fixing its gaze not on itself, but on its object, the Lord Jesus.

This does not come naturally, though, not even for seasoned ministers of the word. That is why all Christians, even pastors, need to hear good news, for the gospel strengthens our faith. Near the end of his life, as he battled blindness and physical weakness, the Reformed theologian Robert Dabney (1820–1898) began to do what we all do from time to time: he began looking inward to his own sins and afflictions rather than outward to Christ. Wavering in his faith, he wrote to his old friend Clement Read Vaughn, confessing that he was not sure that his faith would be strong enough to face death. Vaughn replied to Dabney in a written letter that has survived as a sterling example of a friend pointing another friend to

Jesus Christ. Vaughn asked Dabney what a traveler would do if he came upon a canyon over which a bridge was built:

> What does he do to breed confidence in the bridge? He looks at the bridge; he gets down and examines it. He doesn't stand at the bridge-head and turn his thoughts curiously in on his own mind to see if he has confidence in the bridge. If his examination of the bridge gives him a certain amount of confidence, and yet he wants more, how does he make his faith grow? Why, in the same way; he still continues to examine the bridge. Now, my dear old man, let your faith take care of itself for a while, and you just think of what you are allowed to trust in. Think of the Master's power, think of his love; think how he is interested in the soul that searches for him, and will not be comforted until he finds him. Think of what he has done, his work. That blood is mightier than all the sins of all the sinners that ever lived. Don't you think it will master yours?
>
> Now, dear old friend, I have done to you just what I would want you to do to me if I were lying in your place. The great theologian, after all, is just like any other one of God's children, and the simple gospel talked to him is just as essential to his comfort as it is to a milk-maid or to a plowboy. May God give you grace not to lay too much stress on your faith, but to grasp the great ground of confidence, Christ, and all his work and all his personal fitness to be a sinner's refuge. Faith is only an eye to see him. I have been praying that God would quiet your pains as you advance, and enable you to see the gladness of the gospel at every step. Good-bye. God be with you as he will. Think of the Bridge!
>
> Your brother,
> C. R. V.[1]

If you want to finish well, think of the Bridge, the Lord Jesus Christ. Anchor your hope in Him, not in your faith or in your performance in the race.

---

1. Thomas Cary Johnson, *The Life and Letters of Robert Lewis Dabney* (Edinburgh: Banner of Truth, 1977), 480.

A Completed Mission

In 4:7, Paul uses three metaphors to describe how God's grace had enabled him to fulfill his ministry and complete his mission. The first is, "I have fought the good fight," an expression that could have either military or athletic connotations. The apostle's point is that the Christian ministry (as well as the entire Christian life) involves a constant struggle against the spiritual forces of darkness. Earlier in this letter, Paul exhorted Timothy, "You therefore must endure hardship as a good soldier of Jesus Christ" (2:3). In his previous letter, he urged Timothy to "wage the good warfare" (1 Tim. 1:18) and "fight the good fight of faith" (6:12). It is a *good* fight because it is fought for the glory of God and His gospel.

Every minister of the word is called to fight this good fight, armed with the gospel of Jesus Christ. "For the weapons of our warfare are not carnal," says Paul to the Corinthians, "but mighty in God for pulling down strongholds, casting down arguments and every high thing that exalts itself against the knowledge of God, bringing every thought into captivity to the obedience of Christ" (2 Cor. 10:4–5). Pastors can be confident that the gospel "is the power of God to salvation for everyone who believes" (Rom. 1:16–17). It announces the promise of eternal life and brings forth the new creation, inaugurated by Jesus (2 Cor. 5:17).

Fighting the good fight, however, is not limited to preaching the gospel and defending the faith in the spiritual battle of competing truth claims (2 Tim. 4:1–5). There is also the subjective element of the fight in the minister's ongoing battle against his own indwelling sin (2:22; cf. 1 Tim. 6:11), as well as the three-headed monster of worry, loneliness, and disappointment (2 Tim. 4:9–16; cf. 2 Cor. 1:8–9; 11:28). Pastors are often hard on themselves for their own failures rather than resting in the absolution they receive through Christ's blood and the acceptance that is theirs through His righteousness. They frequently feel isolated by life as a role model for the flock, having very few friends (if any at all) with whom they can speak honestly. Their families often suffer from controversies in the church and the gossip and misbehavior of some of its members. In other vocations (such as a doctor, lawyer, or president of the United States) moral failure is not an immediate disqualification, but in the Christian ministry, rarely is it not. Seeking to cope with these pressures, some men in the ministry turn to artificial and unhealthy methods of self-medicating, such as pornography, substance abuse, or overeating. Rather than fighting the three-headed monster vigilantly, it is simply avoided.

So how can a minister fight the good fight? To find the answer, we must consider the apostle Paul. What did he do? He continued to find his strength for the fight "in the grace that is in Christ Jesus" (2 Tim. 2:1). Delighting in the gospel, he continued to preach the gospel (Rom. 1:14–16; 1 Cor. 9:16). He often felt weak, but he discovered that in his weakness, Christ's power is made perfect (2 Cor. 12:9). He armed himself with the armor of God so that he could stand against the schemes of the devil (Eph. 6:11). He did not neglect prayer (Acts 16:25; Eph. 6:18–19; 1 Thess. 5:17) nor the comfort of Christian fellowship (Rom. 1:11; 15:24; Phil. 1:8; 1 Thess. 3:6; 2 Tim. 1:4). He was able to rejoice always in Christ (Phil. 4:4) and learned in whatever situation to find his contentment in Him (Phil. 4:11–13; 1 Tim. 6:6).

Paul's second description of his fulfilled ministry is "I have finished the race" (2 Tim. 4:7). Some years earlier on the shores of Miletus, while he prepared to board a ship that was bound for Jerusalem, Paul addressed the elders of the Ephesian church for the last time in person (Acts 20:17–38). He declared his goal to finish his race: "But none of these things move me; nor do I count my life dear to myself, so that I may finish my race with joy, and the ministry which I received from the Lord Jesus, to testify to the gospel of the grace of God" (v. 24). Now, at the end of his life, by the grace of God, he was able to say that he had completed his race. He makes no claim to have won the race; he was simply content to cross the finish line.

So it should be for every Christian pastor. It is often the case that younger men, on completing seminary and entering the ministry, dream of doing great things for the church. Nowadays, many pastors are tempted to measure their value (as well as that of others) by the size of their congregation, number of published books and podcast listeners, and the possession of a PhD. But we must remember that the race we have been given to run is not a competition. Christ, "the righteous Judge" (2 Tim. 4:8), is not looking for the runner with the fastest time or most popularity. Recognition by others does not count for anything in this race. Rather, Christ wants runners who will remain dependent on His grace, enduring to the end.

In his book *Pastoral Theology: The Pastor in the Various Duties of His Office*, Thomas Murphy issued a sobering warning to ambitious pastors:

> All other motives than the constraining love of Christ in the heart soon lose their influence. There are no doubt other incentives, such as ambition, love of learning and desire for social influence, that may carry forward a minister for a while with apparent pleasure. But they will not stand the wear and tear of years of drudgery and trial. If the pastor who is chiefly actuated by these is successful, they will soon satiate; if he is not as successful as he expected to be, he becomes discouraged and disgusted with his office. If there is nothing more than these, the ministry soon becomes a miserable failure. But when the love of Christ reigns in the heart supremely, it gives an impulse to the whole life that is ever steady and joyous. The wear and tear of toiling years will not wear it out. Sometimes there may appear only little success, but it has a faith that lays hold of the promises and is not discouraged. Through prosperity or adversity, among friends or enemies, in failing or continuing health, it moves steadily forward, impelled by an inward affection that cannot be quenched.[2]

Paul does not tell Timothy, "Go do great things for God." Instead he says, "But you be watchful in all things, endure afflictions, do the work of an evangelist, fulfill your ministry" (4:5). Christ has already

2. Murphy, *Pastoral Theology*, 24–25.

won the race. The rest of us are simply called to stay the course and finish without dropping out or becoming disqualified.

Paul's third affirmation about the completion of his service is, "I have kept the faith" (4:7). He had faithfully guarded the good deposit entrusted to him and was now passing the torch to Timothy and the next generation. "The faith" (note the definite article) is a reference to the gospel and essential Christian doctrine. Paul has already warned Timothy in this letter about those who have "strayed concerning the truth" (2:18) and are "disapproved concerning the faith" (3:8). Now Timothy must live according to the example of his spiritual father and keep the faith to the end. This is in accordance with Paul's earlier exhortation: "Hold fast the pattern of sound words which you have heard from me" and "that good thing which was committed to you, keep by the Holy Spirit who dwells in us" (1:13, 14).

Sadly, some ministers have failed to finish the race because they embraced false teaching and did not keep the faith. Some have abandoned the faith altogether, kissing Christianity goodbye. The church needs faithful ministers of the word who will guard the purity of the gospel and apostolic doctrine, bringing it into the next generation.

There is a wider application of 4:7, however, to all believers. The call to fighting the good fight, finishing the race, and keeping the faith is not limited to ordained ministers. In one sense, all believers are called to this. We have a fight to fight. A real spiritual war is being waged, one in which the people of God are engaged. All Christian men and women are to "put on the whole armor of God," as Paul said to the church at Ephesus, so that we may "be able to stand against the wiles of the devil. For we do not wrestle against flesh and blood, but against principalities, against powers, against the rulers of the darkness of this age, against spiritual hosts of wickedness in the heavenly places" (Eph. 6:11–12). We have a race to run. Hebrews 12:1–2 tells us, "Therefore we also, since we are surrounded by so great a cloud of witnesses, let us lay aside every weight, and the sin which so easily ensnares us, and let us run with endurance the race that is set before us, looking unto Jesus, the author and finisher of our faith, who for the joy that was set before Him endured the cross, despising the shame, and has sat down at the right hand of the throne of God." And we have the faith to keep, for which we must contend earnestly (Jude 3). We are to stand together "in one spirit, with one mind striving together for the faith of the gospel" (Phil. 1:27). The promise of Jesus is that in doing these things, He will give us rest for our weary souls (Matt. 11:28–30) and reward us in His grace.

An Anticipated Reward

In 2 Timothy 4:8, Paul rejoices in what awaits him: "Finally, there is laid up for me the crown of righteousness, which the Lord, the righteous Judge, will give to me on that Day." In the Olympic games of the ancient world, wreaths of honor were placed on the heads of winners like crowns. Here, Paul uses the metaphor of a "crown of righteousness" to describe the permanent and perfect state of righteousness that will be ours in glory. This is the righteousness that Christ earned for us through His active obedience to the Father. It has already been imputed to the sinner who trusts in Christ. God justifies and declares righteous all those who receive this righteousness by faith (Rom 3:21–26; 4:5; 5:1; Gal. 2:16–21; 3:10–14). Nevertheless, justified believers are not yet glorified. Although God already regards the believer as righteous on account of the imputed righteousness of Christ, He has not yet brought the believer to completion. In this life, we are still undergoing the slow, lifelong process of being sanctified—that is, made more righteous internally. We long for our sanctification to be complete, and we wait for that day when we will be glorified and enjoy perfect righteousness, in both body and soul. This is the crown of righteousness that Paul says is laid up for him. It is that great inheritance that Peter describes as "incorruptible and undefiled and that does not fade away, reserved in heaven for you" (1 Peter 1:4).

This reward is not for the apostle Paul alone, but for every believer in the Lord Jesus Christ. Paul adds, "And not to me only but also to all who have loved His appearing" (2 Tim. 4:8). The same crown of righteousness that awaited Paul also awaited Timothy. And it awaits you too, Christian. Do you love the appearing of Christ? Do you rejoice in what He accomplished through His life, death, and resurrection during His first coming? Are you longing for His return when He will destroy death forever, annihilate all evil, and raise our bodies from the dead to live in eternal, glorified life? If so, the crown of righteousness awaits you at the end of your race. Press on! Don't give up!

It is only because of Jesus that we will receive the crown of righteousness. We are winners of the race because of Him. Jesus fought the good fight perfectly, fulfilling all the righteous demands of God's law through His active obedience to the Father. He loved His neighbor impeccably, resisted temptation unwaveringly, and conquered Satan decisively. At the end of His life he was able to say to the Father, "I have glorified You on the earth. I have finished the work which You have given Me to do. And now, O Father, glorify Me together with Yourself, with the glory which I had with You before the world was" (John 17:4–5). The next day, as He hung on the cross and suffered the wrath of God for the sins of those whom the Father gave Him, He cried out as He died, "It is finished!" (19:30). He completed His mission. He won the race for us. The crown of righteousness, therefore, is a gift of grace from beginning to end.

What consolation and encouragement this brings us as those who find ourselves troubled in conscience by the weakness of our faith and our failures in the Christian life. In His life, death, and resurrection, Jesus was our legal representative and earned the merit we needed to be acceptable to God. The victory is ours because of Christ. God accepts us and loves us not because of how well we are fighting the good fight and running the race, but because of how well His Son did. What comfort this brings to those who feel weak in the fight and weary in the race! This good news strengthens us to fight the good fight and finish the race, looking always to Jesus. For in Him, we are already victorious. This is the key to finding the motivation and encouragement we need to keep going: look to Christ! "In Christ," said Ambrose, "we have everything.... If you find yourself oppressed by guilt, He is your righteousness. If you are in need of help, He is your strength. If you are afraid of death, He is the life. If you desire heaven, He is the way. If you need refuge from the darkness, He is the light."[3] May God strengthen us by His grace so that we too may run hard and finish well.

---

3. Ambrose, *Preghiere*, ed. Inos Biffi (Casale Monferrato, Italy: Piemme, 1987), 16–17. Translation mine.

13

Safely into His Heavenly Kingdom

2 TIMOTHY 4:9–22

Be diligent to come to me quickly; for Demas has forsaken me, having loved this present world, and has departed for Thessalonica—Crescens for Galatia, Titus for Dalmatia. Only Luke is with me. Get Mark and bring him with you, for he is useful to me for ministry. And Tychicus I have sent to Ephesus. Bring the cloak that I left with Carpus at Troas when you come—and the books, especially the parchments.

Alexander the coppersmith did me much harm. May the Lord repay him according to his works. You also must beware of him, for he has greatly resisted our words.

At my first defense no one stood with me, but all forsook me. May it not be charged against them.

But the Lord stood with me and strengthened me, so that the message might be preached fully through me, and that all the Gentiles might hear. Also I was delivered out of the mouth of the lion. And the Lord will deliver me from every evil work and preserve me for His heavenly kingdom. To Him be glory forever and ever. Amen!

Greet Prisca and Aquila, and the household of Onesiphorus. Erastus stayed in Corinth, but Trophimus I have left in Miletus sick.

Do your utmost to come before winter.

Eubulus greets you, as well as Pudens, Linus, Claudia, and all the brethren.

The Lord Jesus Christ be with your spirit. Grace be with you. Amen.

The final verses of 2 Timothy provide us with a window into the life of the apostle Paul unlike any other part of Scripture. These are his last surviving words. Here we see him as he was just before his death: incarcerated, uncomfortable, and lonely. By God's grace, he did not lose his faith in Christ, his hope in the resurrection, or his love for the church. He was able to say, "I have fought the good fight, I have finished the race, I have kept the faith" (4:7). Yet he was also suffering in prison. He had been deeply wounded by a trusted friend, attacked by a bitter enemy, and oppressed by a less-than-perfect government. He longed for the fellowship of his colleagues in the ministry. He yearned for the comfort of a warm coat and a few books.

It is a fascinating glimpse of Paul, especially when we consider the giant that he was. This is the same man who for thirty years never stopped preaching the gospel. He made several dangerous missionary journeys, planting churches throughout the Mediterranean, Asia, and Europe. He wrote what are arguably the deepest and most profound books of the New Testament. He was caught up to the third heaven and given a vision too glorious for words. He defended the gospel before Jewish leaders in countless synagogues. He preached Christ to some of the world's greatest thinkers at Mars Hill. He testified of the truth before powerful kings and governors. He bore scars from receiving the deadly thirty-nine lashes five times and beatings with rods three times. He had been shipwrecked, stoned, left for dead, and he was in danger and difficulty more times than he could probably remember. If any follower of Jesus embodied the titles of "good soldier," "athlete," and "hard-working farmer" (2:3–6 ESV) it was the apostle Paul. He was a legendary figure, a champion for the Christian faith.

Yet in his final words to Timothy, we see someone who is merely human and mortal, just like us. Paul's laments at the end of his letter are not the pitiful words of a man feeling sorry for himself. These are the open and honest remarks from one friend to another. Reading this passage, we discover the source of Paul's strength while he suffered. Like every Christian, Paul had to rely on the grace of God to persevere to the end. He looked to the Lord to bring him safely into His heavenly kingdom, even though he had been deserted by friends, attacked by enemies, and oppressed by the state.

Deserted by Friends

"Be diligent to come to me quickly," Paul says in 4:9. His impending death (4:6) made the request urgent. Paul did not expect to be released. He was certain that he would soon depart this life and be brought into Christ's heavenly kingdom (4:18). He hoped to see his faithful coworker one more time before he died. He was lonely and a little heartbroken: "For Demas has forsaken me, having loved this present world, and has departed for Thessalonica" (4:10).

Demas is mentioned three times in the New Testament: once at the end of Paul's letter to the Colossians (Col. 4:14); again at the end of his letter to Philemon (Philemon 24); and here, at the end of his second letter to Timothy (4:10). He was one of Paul's "fellow laborers" (Philemon 24), an ordained minister of the gospel. This is why his desertion was so painful to Paul. Demas was a trusted colleague. He was more than an acquaintance; he was a coworker in the ministry of the word. He was a companion with whom Paul prayed, preached, taught, and traveled. He was part of the brotherhood of pastors, men who know firsthand what it means to agonize over souls and to have their own souls poured out for the sake of the gospel. And yet Demas had walked away from the ministry, if not the faith altogether.

Paul censures Demas by saying that he "loved this present world." The Greek word translated "world" (*aiōna*) means "age." Paul viewed the world through the lens of two ages: the present age and the age to come. The present age, which began with Adam's fall, is characterized by sin, sorrow, and death. The age to come, which will be consummated at the return of Christ, is characterized by righteousness, joy, and life. Christians do not belong to the present age, for it is an "evil age" (Gal. 1:4) whose god is Satan (2 Cor. 4:4). They belong to the age to come, which has already been inaugurated (though not yet consummated) with the resurrection and ascension of Christ.

Although a Christian lives in both of these ages simultaneously and experiences the inner conflict of being concurrently justified and sinful, he cannot be *in love* with both of these ages. "If anyone loves the world, the love of the Father is not in him" (1 John 2:15b). Either we love this present evil age and want it to continue or we long for the return of Christ, which will bring this age to an end. Because believers do not belong to this present evil age, they are not to be conformed to it. Paul writes in Romans 12:2: "And do not be conformed to this world, but be transformed by the renewing of your mind." Sadly, his colleague in the ministry had done just the opposite. In love with this present age, Demas deserted Paul and went to Thessalonica, indicating that his love for Christ had grown cold.

In addition to Demas's desertion, other colleagues of Paul had left him in order to serve the needs of churches. Crescens (mentioned only here in the New Testament, 4:10) had gone to Galatia; and Titus, the minister serving the church on Crete, had gone to Dalmatia, which is located in southern Illyricum, across the Adriatic Sea from southern Italy. Tychicus (4:12), whom Paul describes elsewhere as "a beloved brother and faithful minister in the Lord" (Eph. 6:21–22; cf. Col. 4:7–8; Titus 3:12), had been sent to Ephesus, possibly to carry this letter to Timothy and serve the church there while Timothy visited Paul in Rome. The apostle does not censure these three men, but he certainly misses their company.

These transparent remarks by Paul remind us of our basic need for friends. God did not intend for humans to go through life alone. He designed us to live in the companionship of family and friends. We are made in the image of the triune God, who lives in the perfect community of the divine persons: Father, Son, and Holy Spirit. Just as none of the persons of the Godhead exist independently of the other two, neither do God's image bearers exist independently of other image bearers. This is one of the reasons why God said in the beginning that it is not good for the man to be alone. Isolation and loneliness are destructive enemies. We need others. This basic human need weighed heavily on the apostle Paul as he was imprisoned and deserted by friends. John Stott observes,

> We must not play down the urgency of Paul's affectionate desire to see Timothy. The same apostle who has set his love and hope upon the coming of Christ, nevertheless also longs

> to see Timothy.... The two longings are not incompatible. One sometimes meets super-spiritual people who claim that they never feel lonely and have no need of human friends, for the companionship of Christ satisfies all their needs. But human friendship is the loving provision of God for mankind.[1]

Notice how the Lord strengthened Paul through human friendship. Although he bore the pain of Demas's desertion as well as those in Asia who turned away from him (2 Tim. 1:15), Paul was comforted by the presence of Luke (4:11a). He was also well aware that there were believers in Ephesus and many other places who loved him and were praying for him. "Greet Prisca and Aquila, and the household of Onesiphorus" (4:19). Prisca and Aquila were the husband-and-wife team with whom he stayed and worked in Corinth (Acts 18:1–3), who later accompanied him to Ephesus (vv. 18–22), where Timothy currently ministered. Onesiphorus was the same man whom Paul commends in 2 Timothy 1:16–18. Paul sends his warm greetings to Onesiphorus's family, as well as to his dear friends Prisca and Aquila, because he loves them and appreciates their service to him.

Paul also tells Timothy to "get Mark and bring him with you, for he is useful to me for ministry" (4:11b). This Mark is undoubtedly the same man who accompanied Paul and Barnabas on their first missionary journey (Acts 12:25; 13:5, 13). There was a time, many years earlier, when Mark had deserted Paul, leading to the sharp disagreement between Paul and Barnabas (Acts 15:37–40). Later, Mark proved himself as a faithful servant of the church and came to be regarded by Paul as his fellow laborer (Philemon 24; cf. 1 Peter 5:13). Now at the end of his life, Paul asks specifically for Mark. There was no hint of bitterness or resentment toward one who had once deserted him yet later returned.

Strengthened by God's grace, Paul would continue laboring for the gospel, right up to the very end. He asks for his cloak to keep warm and his books to study (2 Tim. 4:13). He provides updates about the mission field: "Erastus stayed in Corinth, but Trophimus

---

1. Stott, *Message of 2 Timothy*, 119–20.

I have left in Miletus sick" (4:20). He urges Timothy to come as quickly as possible and sends greetings from others (4:21). Clearly, even in the midst of his loneliness and sadness, Paul was comforted by the Lord through the companionship and love of others.

Often that is how the Lord works in our lives. He frequently comforts and encourages us through the service, love, and prayers of others. When people reach out to us while we are in affliction, they wear the masks of God. On the surface, Paul saw the ordinary human face of Luke, the one companion who remained with him in his time of need. But beneath Luke's appearance, God was serving Paul, comforting and strengthening him. God had not abandoned him, nor has He abandoned us. He is near us and with us, through the love and service of others.

Perhaps you have been deserted by friends for the sake of Christ. Perhaps you are heartbroken and lonely. But look around. How is God serving you right now through the love and service of particular people? Is there a friend, spouse, relative, or colleague wearing the mask of God? Think of the many ways in which others are serving you. If you are in Christ, God has not deserted you. He is near you, upholding you by His grace, usually in ways that appear very ordinary and insignificant. How might you don the mask of God and serve Him by serving others?

Attacked by Enemies

Not only was Paul deserted by friends but he was also attacked by enemies. In 4:14–15, Paul warns Timothy of an enemy of the gospel, someone who had caused him much pain: "Alexander the coppersmith did me much harm. May the Lord repay him according to his works. You also must beware of him, for he has greatly resisted our words."

It is difficult to identify this man precisely. Alexander was a common name in the first-century Greco-Roman world, and there are several possibilities concerning his identity. He may have been a man in Troas of whom Paul wanted Timothy to beware. Given that Timothy would be stopping in Troas to pick up Paul's coat and books, he should be careful to avoid him. Another possibility is that this was a coppersmith in Rome, where Paul was presently imprisoned. Or this may have been the Alexander in Ephesus who was involved in the infamous riot (Acts 19:33). It seems most likely, though, that this was the same Alexander whom Paul mentions in his first letter to Timothy, the man in Ephesus whom Paul "delivered to Satan," along with Hymenaeus, so that they would learn not to blaspheme (1:20).

Whoever this Alexander was, he had done serious injury to Paul. Paul does not specify the nature of this "great harm," but it seems to have been linked to his arrest and trial. He says in 4:16 that "at my first defense no one stood with me, but all forsook me." Alexander may have brought false testimony against Paul during the first stage of his trial (what Paul refers to as his "first defense"). Paul says this man "greatly resisted our words" (4:15). This was not a fellow Christian with whom Paul had a disagreement. Paul is not expressing an unforgiving heart toward a man with whom he needed to reconcile. Rather, he identifies Alexander as a fierce opponent and bitter foe of the gospel. That is why he warns Timothy to beware of him.

It would have been easy for Paul to complain about what Alexander had done to him. We could probably sympathize with the apostle if he had written a few lines describing what a horrible person Alexander was and how he would like to pay him back. Instead, we see the grace of God at work in Paul and Paul's good example to Timothy. Instead of expressing his anger toward Alexander, Paul took comfort that vengeance belongs to the Lord and that the Lord will have His justice in the end. "May the Lord repay him according to his works" (4:14b).

There is no worse punishment than being repaid by the Lord according to our works. There is nothing more severe than the holy God of eternity satisfying His justice by paying us back for all the sins we have committed against Him. That is the reality of hell and is exactly what will happen to every human being who is not clothed in the righteousness of Christ. Hell is the final destination of every unforgiven sinner and the place where God will have His justice.

Paul is not saying that he wants this judgment to befall Alexander, only that it will unless Alexander repents. Paul knew perfectly well that he was just as deserving of hell as Alexander and that it was only by God's grace in Christ that he had been spared judgment. But he took comfort in the fact that God will have His vengeance, and no one will escape His justice. He is not praying an imprecatory prayer or breathing curses against Alexander. He is simply pointing out that all the wrong done against the gospel—for which he was suffering at the time—will be made right in the end.

Perhaps you have been attacked by enemies of the gospel. Maybe someone has caused you great harm. Are you seeking revenge, or do you take comfort in the fact that the Lord will have His justice in the end? Do you trust God to execute His vengeance, or do you want to rob God of what rightfully belongs to Him by taking matters into your own hands? We would do well to meditate frequently upon Paul's words in Romans 12:

> Bless those who persecute you; bless and do not curse....
>
> Repay no one evil for evil. Have regard for good things in the sight of all men.... Beloved, do not avenge yourselves, but rather give place to wrath; for it is written, "Vengeance is Mine, I will repay," says the Lord. Therefore
>
> > "If your enemy is hungry, feed him;
> > If he is thirsty, give him a drink;
> > For in so doing you will heap coals of fire on his head."
>
> Do not be overcome by evil, but overcome evil with good. (vv. 14, 17, 19–21)

When enemies harm us, instead of retaliating, let us remember that unless that person repents, the Lord will repay him according to his deeds. As the Preacher of Ecclesiastes said at the very end of his book,

> For God will bring every work into judgment,
> Including every secret thing,
> Whether good or evil. (12:14)

It is only because of the certainty of God's justice at the end of history that now, in this life, we can respond with grace and mercy toward those who hurt us.

Oppressed by the State

Paul was not only deserted by friends and attacked by enemies, he was also oppressed by imperfect systems of government. His imprisonment was a miscarriage of justice. He had spent years in custody, from the time of his arrest in Jerusalem, being shuffled from a Roman tribune to the Jewish Council, to the Roman governors Felix and Festus, to Herod Agrippa, and finally to Caesar. Both Festus and Agrippa concluded privately that Paul had done nothing deserving of death or imprisonment (Acts 26:30–32). The charges against him were fabrications by the Jewish religious leaders. Paul's opponents claimed that he was a troublemaker, a revolutionary, and an enemy of Caesar. He appealed to Caesar only to avoid being handed over to the Jews. It was because of the hatred of the Jews and the politics of Rome that Paul had been locked up for years.

Paul notes that when he first stood trial, no one came to his side. Roman law permitted him to call witnesses. Apparently no one among the church at Rome came to help him, "to stand at his side in court either to speak on his behalf, or to advise him in the conduct of his case, or to support him by a demonstration of sympathy."[2] That is why he says in 4:16, "At my first defense no one stood with me, but all forsook me." We cannot be sure why no one came to Paul's defense. Perhaps they were afraid, as the disciples were when Jesus stood trial. Maybe they were negligent and failed to see how Paul needed them at that time. It is also possible that they were embarrassed to be associated with an apostle who was constantly incarcerated. Whatever the case, Paul was left to stand trial alone.

Again, we might understand if Paul were to complain about his situation. If we were in similar circumstances and writing to a close

2. Alfred Plummer, *The Pastoral Epistles*, The Expositor's Bible, ed. W. Robertson Nicoll (Hackette, U. K.: Hodder and Stoughton, 1888), 420.

friend, we might be tempted to grumble. It would be easy to whine about corrupt and incompetent leaders or fellow Christians who had let us down. Once again, though, we do not find Paul doing this. He does not elaborate about the selfishness or cowardice of those who deserted him or about the incompetency or corruption of those in the Roman and Jewish governments. Instead, he speaks about forgiveness. He says emphatically, "May it not be charged against them" (4:16b).

Where did Paul find the power to forgive rather than curse those who had left him to stand trial alone? Only from the Friend who sticks closer than a brother: "But the Lord stood with me and strengthened me" (4:17a). Paul was able to forgive others because he had been forgiven by the Lord. And this same Lord stood by Paul and strengthened him during his imprisonment and trial, "so that the message might be preached fully through [him], and that all the Gentiles might hear" (4:17b). Although Paul's situation looked hopeless, God used these circumstances for the advancement of the gospel.

Safely into His Kingdom

At his first defense, Paul was spared from death. He states that "also I was delivered out of the mouth of the lion" (4:17c). This is not a reference to the lions of the coliseum since Paul, being a Roman citizen, would not have been subjected to such a death. Rather, Paul is using this phrase metaphorically to describe execution. He probably has in mind the attempted execution of Daniel, who, by the grace of God, was spared a violent death while in a den of lions (Daniel 6). Just as Daniel emerged safely from that harrowing experience, Paul had been rescued from the death sentence.

This time, though, there would be no rescue, and Paul knew it. "The time of my departure is at hand," said the aged apostle (4:6). Paul was facing death, and his time on earth was short. Nevertheless, he took courage in God's promise: "And the Lord will deliver me from every evil work and preserve me for His heavenly kingdom" (4:18).

How could Paul speak about God rescuing him from every evil when it was clear that death was certain? How could he be confident that the Lord would preserve him and bring him safely into His kingdom? As a Roman citizen, Paul was facing execution by decapitation. Where was the preservation in that? How could he say that the Lord would rescue him from every evil deed if he was about to face the executioner's sword?

Paul could say this with confidence because of God's promise to raise His people from the dead and bring them to everlasting glory. Paul believed God's promise, "the promise of life which is in Christ Jesus" (2 Tim. 1:1). Because Christ "abolished death and brought life and immortality to light through the gospel" (1:10), Christians have the hope of being brought safely into His heavenly kingdom in the resurrection. While Paul knew that the time of his departure was near, he also knew that God would raise his body from the dead on the last day to dwell on a resurrected earth free from all evil, suffering, and death (cf. Rom. 8:18–25; 1 Cor. 15:20–58; Phil. 3:20–21). No evil deed committed against him could change God's promise or thwart God's purposes. This is why Paul could finish his letter with this great doxology: "To Him be glory forever and ever. Amen!" (4:18b).

This was to be Timothy's model. As the young pastor sought to fulfill his ministry, even amid hardship and persecution, he was to trust God's promises and give God the praise He deserves. This is to be our model as well. As we seek to fulfill our callings as Christians and persevere through trials and suffering, we are to trust God's promises and lift our praises to Him. When we are deserted by friends, attacked by enemies, oppressed by the state, or even facing death, we can, by the power of the Holy Spirit, say, "To Him be glory forever and ever. Amen!" No matter what our situation, we can lift this doxology to Him and be confident that He is in control of all things and deserves all glory for His perfect plans and wisdom.

This is not always easy to do. Sometimes we find it easier to doubt God than to praise Him. When we find ourselves in difficult circumstances, we often think, "Why is God allowing this? If

I had His power, I would change this situation!" We become frustrated with God and forget His promise to bring us safely into His heavenly kingdom. We lose sight of the fact that He will use every evil deed committed against us for His glory and our good. We forget that He will award us the crown of righteousness.

But there is no reason for us to persist in frustration and doubt, for we can be as confident as the great apostle himself that the Lord will keep His promises to us. The same Christ who laid down His life for Paul has also laid down His life for us. And He will stand by us and strengthen us during every trial. We can say with the psalmist:

> The LORD also will be a refuge for the oppressed,
> A refuge in times of trouble.
> And those who know Your name put their trust in You,
> For You, LORD, have not forsaken those who seek you.
> (Ps. 9:9–10)

Jesus had those words on His lips as He underwent suffering. Like Paul, Jesus was deserted by His friends. When He was arrested, His own disciples left him and fled. One even denied Him three times (Luke 22:54–62). Yet unlike Paul, Jesus went to the cross to suffer for the sins of those who deserted Him. "Having loved His own who were in the world, He loved them to the end" (John 13:1). This applies not only to the eleven disciples but to all those whom Christ came to save. For in Adam, all of us have deserted God and deserve His judgment. "All we like sheep have gone astray," says Isaiah; "we have turned, every one, to his own way." But Christ underwent that judgment for us: "and the LORD has laid on Him the iniquity of us all" (Isa. 53:6). By enduring the shame of the cross and the wrath of God for our sake, Jesus showed that "greater love has no one than this, than to lay down one's life for his friends" (John 15:13).

Like Paul, Jesus was attacked by His enemies:

> He is despised and rejected by men,
> A Man of sorrows and acquainted with grief.

And we hid, as it were, our faces from Him;
He was despised, and we did not esteem Him. (Isa. 53:3)

Israel's religious leaders plotted against Jesus, always trying to trap Him in His words. Eventually they bribed one of His disciples to betray Him. They conspired together to arrange for His arrest. They opposed Him at his trial and made false accusations in court. Then, when Jesus was hanging on the cross, they mocked Him, fulfilling the words of Psalm 22:

All those who see Me ridicule Me;
They shoot out the lip, they shake the head, saying,
"He trusted in the LORD, let Him rescue Him;
Let Him deliver Him, since He delights in Him!"...

For dogs have surrounded Me;
The congregation of the wicked has enclosed Me.
They pierced My hands and My feet;
I can count all My bones.
They look and stare at Me.
They divide My garments among them,
And for My clothing they cast lots. (vv.7–8, 16–18)

Jesus suffered these evil deeds and attacks from enemies for our sake, so that we, who once were His enemies, might be reconciled to God (Rom. 5:6–11).

Like Paul, Jesus was oppressed by the state. He was arrested by the authorities, beaten, and wrongly convicted in an illegal court proceeding. Although He was an innocent man, He was sent to His execution. He was tortured by soldiers and crucified as a criminal. As we confess in the ancient creeds, "He suffered under Pontius Pilate" in fulfillment of His submission and obedience to the Father, thereby securing our redemption.

Because Christ suffered desertion, attack, and oppression for us, we can have the confidence that we will be brought safely into the heavenly kingdom. Although our present suffering is evidence that the kingdom of God is not yet consummated, our perseverance is proof that it is already inaugurated. Yes, it is through many tribulations that we must enter the kingdom of God, but God will bring us safely through those tribulations. That is to say, He will not allow your faith to fail or your soul to be lost. He will not give up on you. Therefore, we can praise Him with Paul's doxology in 4:18: "To Him be glory forever and ever. Amen!" And by faith we can joyfully receive God's benediction in 4:22: "The Lord Jesus Christ be with your spirit. Grace be with you."

Anchor your hope in Christ, dear Christian, for He will preserve you and bring you safely into His heavenly kingdom. Amen.